RELATIVELY TRUE

Stories of Truth, Deception,
Post-Truth from the Indian
Subcontinent and Australia

Edited By

Meenakshi Bharat
Sharon Rundle

Orient BlackSwan

RELATIVELY TRUE

ORIENT BLACKSWAN PRIVATE LIMITED

Registered Office
3-6-752 Himayatnagar, Hyderabad 500 029, Telangana, India
E-mail: centraloffice@orientblackswan.com

Other Offices
Bengaluru, Chennai, Guwahati, Hyderabad, Kolkata,
Mumbai, New Delhi, Noida, Patna

First published 2022

ISBN 978 93 5442 305 5

040846

Typeset in Minion Pro 11/13.5 *by*
Shine Graphics, Delhi 110 094

Printed at
Avantika Printers Private Limited, New Delhi 110 020

Published by
Orient Blackswan Private Limited
3-6-752, Himayatnagar, Hyderabad 500 029, Telangana, India
E-mail: info@orientblackswan.com

Contents

Foreword

HE The Hon Barry O'Farrell AO
Australian High Commissioner to India

At the outset, I would like to congratulate Sharon, Meenakshi, all the contributors, and the publishers Orient BlackSwan on the fifth Indo-Australian anthology of short fiction, *Relatively True*.

I hope this anthology will enthral its readers as much as it enthralled me. With its thought-provoking narratives, this collection of short stories explores the underlying human predicament as diverse characters navigate the contemporary realities across cultures and boundaries.

The stories, with all their twists and turns, beautifully draw out that one's truth is entrenched in one's own belief system. As true friends, Australia and India share a common belief system, which is defined by our democratic values and diversity. As we work together to navigate the rapidly changing realities of our world and support each other as critical partners on the international stage, we need to understand each other at multiple levels.

Comprising writings of internationally acclaimed Australian, Indian and diaspora writers, this anthology provides a valuable window into cultures and lives, an understanding as it were of each other's truth. There is no better way of building bridges of understanding and friendship than through stories.

Literature has remained an integral part of the Australian government's public diplomacy engagement in India. In the last few years, we have been strategically working with various stakeholders in India and Australia to highlight the diverse and vibrant voices from both countries. More and more diaspora writers and Indian writers are being read and featured at Australian literary festivals, and vice versa.

In my view, this anthology is a timely and commendable effort in keeping the literary dialogue between Australia and India going, especially in times when physical interactions remain restricted.

Proem

Roanna Gonsalves

In our contemporary world of shallow smiles and deepfakes, of truthiness and viral disinformation, the idea of 'the truth' is a knot that is hard to untangle. We are constantly needing to ask ourselves questions about whom to trust and how much as the boundaries between truth and falsehood are contested unceasingly. When facts fail us, particularly through the constant bombardment with the bogus that we are subjected to in the public spheres of South Asia and Australia, we count on the imagination. We search for the kind of truth that can be most clearly revealed only when clothed in evident untruth. Fiction is the lie that tells us the truth, as many renowned writers have noted. It is fitting, then, that this anthology, *Relatively True*, beautifully explores, through the clarifying and liberatory potential of fiction, those porous borderlands between truth and falsehood, between relativity and rigidity, between that which may be trusted and that which must fall away.

This book is the fifth in a series of remarkable anthologies of short fiction edited by Meenakshi Bharat and Sharon Rundle, each of which explores a theme that is currently resonant in global public discourse. For almost two decades, Bharat and Rundle have steadfastly collaborated across an ocean and two continents to build a body of work that uplifts the voices of so many writers. I have been fortunate to have my work published in two of these anthologies. Though the anthologies feature the work of writers from Australia, India and the rest of South Asia, the creative and intellectual labour held within each book addresses the most pressing concerns of our times across the world.

In a time of increased fracturing of communities and isolation of individuals, be it due to a global pandemic or more personal physical and mental ill health, Bharat and Rundle's anthologies are anticipated with delight. They bring writers together, the great and the emerging, all shoulder-to-shoulder, word-to-word, in the lovingly curated pages of a book. For many of us, it is a privilege to be featured in one of these anthologies for it means our work will be in conversation with readers all over the world and with the work of other writers addressing the same concerns through fiction. This is necessary work, a booster shot, if you like, to guard against simplistic and harmful ideas, to encourage complexity and nuance, to help us understand ourselves and our world.

As I made my way through each story, I was struck by the organisation of this book, attuned as it is to a deepening interrogation of a key concern of our times, that of the idea of 'the truth'. The book seems to eschew an easy spatial or temporal organisational logic. Instead it works with the idea of entanglement, exploring different aspects of truth, half-truths, untruths and obfuscations. In this wonderful anthology, the truth sometimes stands in the way of epiphanies and at other times it is precisely the withholding of information that proves crucial to understanding.

The first section addresses what many of us might first associate with the untruths of our age, the Orwellian notion of doublespeak. Moving from deeply personal relationships to the broader sweep of the idea of the nation, this section coalesces around the use of language and its potential to work as a smokescreen. The section opens with the crisp and clear voice of one of the world's greatest writers, Shirley Hazzard. In Hazzard's 'Flowers of Sorrow', the spuriousness of the official language of work is contrasted with a delicate attunement to beauty and desire, calling to mind our contemporary concerns regarding 'truthiness' and the easy pronouncements of fakery or fake news when information is disagreeable to us. In Eugen Bacon's wonderful work of speculative fiction, 'Unlimited Data', the boundary of the body is transgressed as a consequence of the betrayal of language itself. Gulzar's 'Najoom' tells us a story about destiny, showing us history in a new light. Meenakshi Bharat's insightful work, 'Betrayal', is an exploration of how ideas of nationhood and of truth are distorted through doublespeak.

The second section, 'Fake News', builds on the previous section's exploration of doublespeak to examine the muddying of truth, including through the role of the media and the replication of entrenched interpersonal and societal power dynamics. It opens with Alex Cothren's tragic story 'Let's Talk Trojan Bee', which is artfully constructed out of quotes, building up a particular conception of truth and then providing a takedown of it. This story illustrates the effects of the media's distortion of the truth as well as the idea of pushing the limits of truth too far. In Tony Birch's very engaging satirical work, 'Party Lights', the truth is distorted not just by drugs but especially by the effects of neoliberalism and its attendant class hierarchies. Devika Brendon's superb story, 'Threadbare', explores the idea of imposter syndrome, among other themes. It has many perceptive lines embedded within its nuanced prose. As Brendon's first-person narrator notes, 'in the deep weave of it, the truth resides'. Sharon Rundle's striking work, 'Kiewa Creek Diary', is a meditation upon the obfuscation of truth and the dystopian penalties of the refusal to reveal the truth.

The anthology then turns to the exploration of broader systemic issues related to the loss and gain of power when telling the truth in its third section, 'Dissembling Fraud'. The opening story is the brilliant Cate Kennedy's work 'Direct Action', a moving illumination of truth and the precious value of it to those who matter. In Anne Benjamin's 'Shadow Box', truth is not worth fighting for in a corrupt work environment. In Sujata Sankranti's 'Nothing but the Truth', one gets a sense of a chase between truth and lies, between reversals and denials as the abhorrent practice of casteism is touched upon.

Then in the fourth section, 'Smokescreen', the anthology seems to turn on its head as it begins to question the benefits of always being truthful and offers possibilities around the necessity of deception. This section opens with an excerpt from Kate Grenville's latest historical fiction, *A Room Made of Leaves*, which concerns itself with the replacement of a true history by a false one, the need for pretence in order to survive, the idea of a delicious fantasy, a world where one is ready to wait even for such a thing as a sentence to be revealed. In Priya Sarukkai Chabria's 'Blanket', the truth comes out as an itch, evoking terrible colonial histories associated with blankets and rash. Andrew Kwong's 'The Verdict' revolves around the muddying of truth in the medical profession and the consequences of chasing profit of different kinds, including though insurance claims. Mitra Phukan's insightful 'Wrong Number' illuminates situations where lies and deception can sometimes work for good. There is a movement through deception towards the deeper truth of an epiphany, a realisation unfurling towards new possibilities. Bashabi Fraser's 'My People in Paradise' urges us to question, among other things, our habitual use of language. The lake as a body of water is refreshingly seen as mother, not motherland. Links to the past and to one's people, while unseen and unverifiable, yet keenly felt, are often more comforting than what is visible.

This deepening interrogation of the necessity of telling the truth continues in the fifth section, 'Masquerades and Masks'. This section opens with the esteemed Yasmine Gooneratne's complex story, 'A Little Light Reading', where lies must be told to a husband in order to protect a marriage. Rashida Murphy's 'Talking Beasts' is a splendid, thoughtful reflection upon stretching the truth in order to get what you want. In Sunil Badami's captivating work, 'Something's Gotta Give', simple notions of truth-telling and transparency are skilfully subverted as the consequences of lying to others and lying to oneself propel the narrative into a new understanding of oneself, of what is true deep within.

The sixth and final section, 'Strange Days', unfurls unexpectedly into new ways of thinking about the enmeshment of reality and the imagination, the acceptance of hard truth and the desire to disbelieve it. This final section, rather than offering a simple denouement, an easy unknotting of the ideas explored thus far in the anthology, further ensnares us into considering the sometimes painful, sometimes delicious promise that a rigorous reckoning of reality provides. This section opens with Niharika Chibber Joe and Matt Lupton's 'Heterochromia Iridum', a story that works with creating new truths out of the imagination, new pasts and new futures. Susanne Gervay's 'The Scent of the Ocean' is a compelling story about the 'fracturing between what was real and in their heads'. This enchanting story about the devastating consequences of the lies told by adults to children also explores a world where a child must lie to protect herself, to survive and to emerge anew. In

Janhavi Acharekar's gorgeous story 'Learning to Bake', the baking of a cake symbolises the process of coming to terms with the hard truth about ageing, in the course of rising to meet a realisation. Gayatri Gill's beguiling work, 'The Sweechoos', is a deftly told story exploring the truth about class pretensions, about the use of language, including the hidden meaning of words like 'sweechoo'. The final work is Julia Prendergast's fascinating story 'Today is Tomorrow', a story that invites us, at the close of the anthology, to reconsider easy binaries of truth and falsehood and invites us to 'run' with the narrator who, fittingly, for a story that speaks so insistently and clearly to our current historical moment, is playing with the truth of time.

In our uncertain and precarious times, *Relatively True* offers an illuminating exploration of the different ways in which we might think about the idea of 'the truth', the dangers it poses as well as the possibilities it affords. This wondrous collection of some of the best stories from Australia and South Asia is a timely offering that enchants, provokes and enlightens, from the first story to the last, as it asks us to explore the knot, to reconsider what we once may have thought was 'the truth'.

Introduction

Pushing Truth

Meenakshi Bharat and Sharon Rundle

Acts of lying, dissembling, pussyfooting, prevaricating, counterfeiting, fudging, and whitewashing are not new. Trickster stories abound in all ancient cultures. Indeed, the luscious, juicy apple that enticed Eve points to an originary streak of deception that is endemic to humankind. So, Sita in Valmiki's *Ramayana* was beguiled by the vision of a golden deer—in reality, Marich the demon, conscripted by Ravan the Lankan king. So also did the lovely Lady Macbeth exhort her husband to 'look like the innocent flower, / But be the serpent under 't'.

But in recent years, the deliberateness of deception has been taken to quite another level. The mantra of fakery not only imbues day-to-day dealings between individuals, but has also become the way nations and peoples engage with each other. Truth is obfuscated; it becomes relative. In today's world, the internet and social media conspire to disseminate half-truths, paranoia, clickbait, rumour, and gossip. In this environment of elastic truth, fake identities rule the roost, infiltrating dating sites, job-seeking sites, personal profiles, photos, and CVs. Cleverly enhanced photos of real estate and property descriptions project tempting scenarios of a perfect lifestyle. Nothing is what it seems.

Facts are challenged. Science is ridiculed. Opinions and beliefs are elevated, clamouring to be given equal time and weight in discussions. Myriad conspiracy theories are circulated. A rumour in the stock market sends economies crashing. Smear campaigns cut short promising careers. Online trolling can have severe consequences for its targets. Innumerable manifestations of manipulation abound—leaders lie, conceal and manoeuvre the truth; corporations create fantasies through advertising; close friends, neighbours and family may be living lives of deception or self-deception. Distressingly, we, ourselves, may have taken part in one or the other of these manipulations. The line between lies and the truth has become wafer-thin. Even seemingly innocent everyday actions like making a kind but not necessarily true statement, or wearing make-up, or being cagey about one's age become dubious—almost lies.

On the one hand, we are fortunate to have constant and immediate access to information. On the other hand, the overwhelming deluge of available information only adds to the mounting confusion, encouraging selective skimming and severely impacting comprehension. The easier it is to access information, the harder it is to sift through it to access the facts. And the more we hear something, the more we are inclined to believe it as true—the illusion-of-truth effect. But, as Gandhi averred, 'An error does not become truth by reason of multiplied propagation'. Equally, he had continued, truth does not 'become error because nobody sees it'.

In this scenario, truth becomes elusive. Indeed, our lexicon itself has changed under the vitiating drive of a new compulsive, concerted pseudo-religion of fakery to give currency to terms like 'post-truth'. This idea of post-truth has a frightening relativity which makes truth itself susceptible to the notion of falsity and fakery. While we ponder on whose truth is relevant and meaningful—yours or mine—we have lost sight of values which now seem suspect. White lies, bending the truth, using flattery to enhance social and employment prospects, presenting picture-perfect visions of our lives and families—these colour our perception of truth both in our private and public existences. The way we see the truth in politics, government, parliament, and institutions has a major impact on us as citizens. In this scenario, whom do we trust? Or worse, in this set-up, can we trust at all?

The stories in this, our fifth collection of Indo-Australian short fiction, *Relatively True*, confront and address these questions, and more, in surprising and creative ways. Each narrative, in its own inimitable way, probes the vexing impact of the now fluctuating ideas of truth and deception on us, as individuals and, in a wider sense, as part of a community and of humanity. In fact, the stories collectively identify a critical truth: narratives invigorate and sustain humanity. Narratives are the medium through which we present ourselves and interpret the world around us. It is through narratives that we learn the unique truth about ourselves and our world. It is through stories that we are pointed to the one everlasting truth of life—that *Truth does matter.*

The stories that we have gathered here are driven by this abiding idea. If the deceiving British claim of terra nullius proves itself to be a weak foundational principle of modern Australia, then the Uluru Statement from the Heart comes as a generous true initiative by Indigenous Australians to unite the Australian people in the idea of a stronger nation. Yet, even as this saving notion is enunciated, it excites detractors to come up with quick denials, and to rake up rumours and conspiracies while issuing dire warnings. Our stories attempt to break through the smokescreen of manipulation at all levels; to weigh when lies become 'the truth' and to ascertain the 'real truth' behind these lies. The effort needs to be made, for, to quote Gandhi once again, 'Even if you are a minority of one, the truth is the truth… Truth stands, even if there be no public support. It is self-sustained.'

Doublespeak

The Flowers of Sorrow

Shirley Hazzard

'In my country', the great man said, looking out over hundreds of uplifted faces, 'we have a song that asks, "Will the flowers of joy ever equal the flowers of sorrow?"'

The speech, up to then, had been the customary exhortation—to uphold the Organisation, to apply oneself unsparingly to one's work—and this made for an interesting change. Words like 'joy' and, more especially, 'sorrow' did not often find their way into that auditorium, and were particularly unlooked-for on Staff Day when the Organisation was at its most impersonal. The lifted faces—faces of a certain fatigued assiduity whose contours, dinted with the pressure of administrative detail, suggested habitual submergence beneath a flow of speeches such as this—responded with a faint, corporate quiver. Members of the staff who had been half sleeping when the words reached them were startled into little delayed actions of surprise, and blew their noses or put on their glasses—to show they had been listening. In the galleries, throats were cleared and legs recrossed. The interpreters' voices hesitated in the earphones, then accelerated to take in this departure from the Director-General's prepared text. 'Les fleurs du chagrin', said the pretty girl in Booth No 2; 'Las flores del dolor', said the Spanish interpreter, with a shrug toward his assistant.

The man on the rostrum now repeated the words from the song, in his own language—and apparently for his own satisfaction, since throughout the hall only a few very blond heads nodded comprehendingly. He went on in English. 'Perhaps', he said, 'perhaps the answer to that question is No.' Now there was a long pause. 'But we should remember that sorrow does produce flowers of its own. It is a misunderstanding always to look for joy. One's aim, rather, should be to conduct oneself so that one need never compromise one's secret integrity; so that even our sufferings may enrich us—enrich us, perhaps, most of all.' He had laid his hand across his mimeographed text, which was open at the last page, and for a moment it seemed that he meant to end the speech there. The précis-writers were still scribbling 'our sufferings may enrich us'. However, he looked down, shifted his hand, and went on. He thanked them all for continued devotion to their duties in the past year, and for the productivity illustrated by an increased flow of documentation in the five official languages. There would be no salary raise this year for the Subsidiary Category. The Pension Plan was under review by a newly appointed working group, and the proposed life-insurance scheme would be studied by an impartial committee. It was hoped to extend recreational facilities along the lines recommended by the staff representatives... He greatly looked forward to another such meeting with the staff before long.

The speaker stood a few moments with his speech in his hand, inclined his head politely to applause, and withdrew.

In the eyes of the world he was a personality—fearless, virtuous, remote—and the ovation continued a little longer without reference to the content of the speech, although some staff members were already filing out and others had begun their complaints while still applauding.

'Scarcely a mention of the proposed change in retirement age.' A burly Belgian youth from Forms Control gave a last angry clap as he moved into the aisle. 'And not a word about longevity increments.' This he said quite fiercely to a Canadian woman, Clelia Kingslake, who had a modest but unique reputation for submitting reports in advance of deadlines.

'That might come under the pension review', she suggested.

'He would have said so. It's just a move to hold the whole thing over for another year.' He held the heavy glass exit door for her. The vast hallway into which they passed was brightly lit, and thickly carpeted in a golf-links green. 'And what in God's name was all that about flowers?'

They were joined by Mr Matta from Economic Cooperation. 'Yes, what was that?' Mr Matta, from the Punjab, had a high lilting voice like a Welshman's and often omitted the article. 'Has D-G gone off his head, I wonder?'

A group passed them heading for the elevators. Someone said violently, '... not even on the agenda!'

When they arrived at the escalator leading to the cafeteria, Miss Kingslake asked the two men, 'Are you coming up for tea?'

'Maybe later', said the Belgian boy. 'Must go back to the office and see what's come in with the afternoon distribution.'

'Back to the shop, I'm afraid', said Mr Matta from Economic Cooperation. 'Our workload has reached the point of boiling.'

Clelia Kingslake, who had greying hair and a light-grey dress, got on the moving stair alone and went up to the cafeteria.

The cafeteria was full. It usually was—and invariably after a staff meeting. Miss Kingslake joined the queue and when her turn came took a tray from the rack and a fork and spoon from the row of metal boxes. First there was a delay (someone ahead was buying containers of coffee for an entire office—a breach of good faith), and then the line moved along so quickly that she found herself at the cake before she had decided what to have. She would have preferred a single piece of bread with jam, but she had passed the butter and it would have been unthinkable to go back for it. So she took down from the glass shelf what seemed to be the largest piece of cake there. A sweet-faced Spanish woman at the tea counter fixed her up with a cup of boiling water and a tea bag, and she paid.

She wandered out into the centre of the room looking for an empty table. There did not seem to be one, and certainly not one by the windows on the river side. She moved along beside the tables with the unfocused, purposeful step of a sleep-walker. Hot water spilled over into the saucer of her cup.

'Miss Kingslake. Miss Kingslake.'

'Oh, Mr Willoughby.'

'I've got a table at the window, if someone hasn't taken it.'

'I thought you'd gone to the Field. I heard your assignment to mission went through.'

'I leave tomorrow night. But not for Santiago after all. That was changed. Let me have your tray. They're sending me to Kuala Lumpur.'

'Thanks, but I'd better not let go. I hadn't heard.'

They made their way through to the windows. She balanced her tray on a corner of his table while he cleared it of the cups, plates, and teabags discarded by the previous occupants. When he had stacked these on the heating equipment, they sat down.

Claude Willoughby was a spare, fair-haired Anglo-Saxon who resembled nothing so much as a spar of bleached wood washed up on a beach. He was, for so industrious a man, remarkably able. He and Clelia Kingslake had been thrown together in Interim Reports, before her upgrading to Annual Reports and his lateral transfer to the World Commodity Index.

'I might—' he began.

She said at the same moment, 'I'm so glad—'

They both said, 'I'm sorry. '

'You might?' she inquired, squeezing her teabag and putting it in the ashtray.

'I was going to say that I might have inquired whether you really wanted to join me. You seemed to be in a trance.'

'I was afraid of seeing someone I didn't want to sit with. Instead, what a nice surprise.' She took two paper napkins from the metal dispenser on the table, and gave him one.

'You were going to say?' he asked. 'Something about being glad?'

'How glad I am, that's all, to see you before you go. I thought you must have left without saying goodbye.'

'I've been terribly busy. Forms, clearances, briefing—and of course my replacement hasn't even been appointed. They're holding the post for an African candidate—or so I'm told. And then, at home—you can imagine—all the packing and storing, added to which we've already taken the children out of school.' Mr Willoughby, having four children of school age, was a substantial beneficiary of the Staff Education Grant. 'But don't let's get into that. And of course I wouldn't have gone without saying goodbye.'

When he had said this, she stared out the window and he turned his head toward the next table, where two officials of the Department of Personnel were getting up from their coffee.

'Shouldn't have said that about the flowers', one of them remarked—a ginger-haired Dutchman in charge of Clerical Deployment. 'Unnecessary.'

'I should think', agreed his friend, Mr Andrada from Legal Aspects. 'If I may say so, not good for morale.'

'Particularly that part about the answer being No.'

'Isn't it curious', Mr Willoughby said to Miss Kingslake, 'how uneasy people are made by any show of feeling in official quarters?' He placed his paper napkin under his cup to absorb spilt tea. 'I suppose they find it inconsistent. What did you think of those remarks today—I mean, about the flowers?'

Miss Kingslake was still looking out at the broad river and the wasteland of factories on its opposite bank. She held the teacup in both hands, her elbows on the table. 'I don't quite know. I think I felt heartened to hear something said merely because it was felt. Something that—wasn't even on the agenda. Still, I did find all that stuff about one's integrity a bit Nordic. After all, it would hardly be possible for most people to get through a working day without compromising their idea of themselves.'

'I think he said "*secret* integrity".' Mr Willoughby drank his tea. 'We can check it tomorrow in the Provisional Verbatim Record.'

'I suppose', she conceded, 'it would depend on how secret one was prepared to let it become.'

The noise in the cafeteria, like that of a great storm, was beyond all possibility of complaint or remedy. It was a noise in some ways restful to staff members from quiet offices, and Clelia Kingslake was one of these. Eating her cake with a fork, resting her cheek on her left hand, she looked quite at ease—more at ease, in fact, than was appropriate to her type.

'You busy at present?' Mr Willoughby asked her.

'Oh yes', she said. (It was a question which had never in the Organisation's history been known to meet with a negative reply.) 'We're finishing up the report on Methods of Enforcement.'

'How is it this year?'

'A much stronger preamble than the last issue. And some pretty tough recommendations in Appendix III.'

Someone leaned over their table. 'You using this chair?'

A group of the interpreters had come in. The interpreters were always objects of interest, their work implying an immediacy denied to the rest of the staff. They stacked their manila folders on the heaters and pushed up extra chairs to the table vacated by the officers of Personnel. Two of them went to fetch tea for the entire table. The rest sat down and began to talk loudly, like children let out of the examination room.

'One could see something was coming when he looked up like that.'

'Les fleurs du chagrin... I suppose one could hardly have said Les fleurs du mal...'

A Russian came back with a loaded tray. 'What are you laughing at?'

One of the English interpreters said, 'It would be better not to give us a prepared text at all than to make all these departures from it.'

'What did you think of the speech?' Mr Willoughby asked a white-haired Frenchman who paused to greet him.

'Most interesting.' Mr Raymond-Guiton bowed to Miss Kingslake over his tray. 'And particularly well calculated—that interpolation about the flowers.'

Miss Kingslake said, 'I rather thought that seemed extempore.'

Mr Raymond-Guiton smiled. 'Most interesting.' The repetition of the remark had the effect of diminishing its significance. He passed on with his tray and disappeared behind a screen of latticed plants.

'Now wasn't it he', Miss Kingslake asked, wrinkling up her brow, 'who refused to go to the Bastille Day party because of his aristocratic connections?'

'You're thinking of that fat chap in the Development Section. This one's too well-bred to do a thing like that. Miss Kingslake, shall we go?'

No sooner had they risen from their chairs than two pale girls in short skirts came up with their trays of tea and cake and started to push the empty dishes aside. Miss Kingslake and Mr Willoughby lost one another briefly in the maze of tables and met again outside the glass doors, in the relative shelter of a magazine stand.

'May I see you to your elevator bank, Miss Kingslake?'

'That would be lovely', she said.

They went down a short flight of steps and walked slowly along a grey-tiled, grey-walled corridor lined with blue doors.

'I wonder', she said, 'if we will ever meet again.'

'I have been wondering that too', he answered without surprise. 'In a place like this there are so many partings and reunions—yet one does find one's way back to the same people again. Rather like those folk dances they organise at Christmas in the Social and Anthropological Department. I feel we shall meet.'

They reached a row of elevator doors. Mr Willoughby pushed the Up button.

She said, as if they were on a railway platform, 'Don't wait.'

'I really should get back to the office', he said, 'and see if my Travel Authorisation's come in yet.'

'Of course.'

'Shall we say goodbye, then?'

'Why yes', she said, but did not say goodbye.

A Down elevator stopped but no one got off. A messenger boy went slowly past wheeling a trolley of stiff brown envelopes.

'Miss Kingslake', Mr Willoughby said. 'Miss Kingslake. Once, in this corridor, I wanted very much to kiss you.'

She stood with her back to the grey wall as if she took from it her protective colouring.

He smiled. 'We were on our way to the Advisory Commission on Administrative and Budgetary Questions.'

Now she smiled too, but sadly, clasping her fingers together over the handle of her bag. This prevented him from taking her hand, and he merely nodded his farewell. She had not spoken at all—he had gone quite a way down the corridor before that occurred to her. He was out of sight by the time the elevator arrived.

'Thirty-seven', she announced, getting in.

Someone touched her shoulder. 'So good to see you, Miss Kingslake.' It was Mr Quashie from Archives.

'Oh, Mr Quashie.'

Mr Quashie, wearing a long, light-coloured robe and scrolling a document lightly between his palms, moved up to stand beside her. 'I suppose you were at the meeting?'

'I was, yes.'

'I thought the D-G looked tired.' Mr Quashie stepped aside to let someone get out. 'But then—I hadn't seen him since he addressed the staff last Human Dignity Day.'

'Nor had I.'

'What a job he has. One wonders how anyone stands it. No private life at all. What did you think of the speech, by the way?'

'Quite good. And you?'

'Oh—here's my floor.' Mr Quashie glanced up at the row of lighted numbers. 'I didn't hear much of it. We were busy in the office, and I stayed to answer the phones. Getting off, please. Getting off. And then I took the wrong staircase in the conference building. So I only came in at the very end. I was just in time to hear about the flowers, you know. About how we need more flowers of joy.'

Unlimited Data

Eugen Bacon

'Must have a smartphone', the job ad said.

* * *

For whom does truth exist? Is it there, no matter what, or sometimes possessed by a demon? Perhaps that is why it is twisted. Untruth is straight, a racing stream thirsty for the river. Truth is curvy, a sluggish trudge filled with unease all the way to a peak where air is thin to breathe. He looks with detachment at the lines on his palms, wonders if they are pathways to reality. But, like a slum, it's an existence with no tarmac. Escape is a memory. Just… whose?

* * *

Ping! An assignment alert displayed on the phone.

He was good with gasfitting, roofing, drainage, even power outlets, ladders, testing and repairing. Most electrical things he could do, and gardening. His hands were clever with greenscapes. He could water and feed lilies or stinkwood, trim shrubs or mow grass, fertilise sunflowers or pluck cashews from the plant.

What he wasn't good with was lies. The employer hadn't been upfront at the interview about the data, how it was out of pocket.

* * *

When he closed his eyes, he forgot about poverty. On special occasions, he took his wife Natukunda to the village dance but now there was a toddler in tow, so they could be famous on the red dust a mere fifteen minutes, as laughter drowned out the drums, before baby Mukasa rejected his temporary sitter, often an old woman, and demanded in wailful chorus his mother's breast. And the boy was greedy: he had to expose both tits before he stopped screaming.

Kaikara wished he could see it, how it was before Mukasa, but his eyes were broken, reflections of lost dreams fluttering away with locust wings. He swore he would never do it again, but fate was a tricky thing and a poor man had one solace.

Already Natukunda's bleeding had stopped and her breasts looked tender, even a little swollen. And though the toddler was still suckling, Kaikara suspected his wife was pregnant again, especially with that constipation and her craving for calcium stone, soft as chalk to chew. He reached out a hand to the gods of the mountain and demanded a better explanation.

He was an itinerant handyman on call, peddling over fields, tarmac and potholes, moving from suburb to suburb, gasfitting, roofing, draining, mowing. *Ping!* Another job and he wheeled to it, phone in his pocket. But doing jobs on call gobbled data.

* * *

The black market was in Kabalaga. The wet mire, as he weaved around the slum and its tin roofs, walls made of carton or nylon, told him that the bunch of jobless youths with a prowl of eyes staring at his bicycle were not harmless. They wore jungle shirts and sandals made of tyres.

The programmer he visited demanded a month's wage, the whole six thousand shillings of it. But even that was better than the bundle data deal of 40 MB a day for mobile internet at five hundred shillings, or 25 MB a week for internet everywhere at one thousand, seven hundred and fifty shillings. That is what the employer was offering to slash from Kaikara's wages, leaving him in debt.

He looked at the programmer named Sanyu, like the radio. 'Bluetooth, you say?'

* * *

Natukunda had a stall at the market in Old Kampala. Wood, sticks and sacks held the ramshackle thing together. She sold pineapples, mangoes, watermelons, bananas and jackfruits, sometimes papayas, guavas, sweet potatoes and tomatoes. What she earned was a pittance. But she could buy the occasional gomesi of imported cotton, six metres of it. Rose and lime were her favourite, puffed sleeves brightly coloured, and reaching the floor. Each gomesi fitted her just right, its sash over her hips. When the metres allowed, she made a headdress.

Sometimes she sent money to her parents out east in Mbale. They were always sick with malaria, bilharzia or dysentery, and the witchdoctor's herbs and beheaded cockerel were not working. The old folk needed to walk into a clinic, and the white man's tablets cost money.

Now she looked at her husband, as though he wore empty tins around his leg. 'You're mad, foolish or both', she said. 'Take me back to my parents and they will return your dowry.'

'Crooked wood shows the best sculptor. The programmer is working with nature. His invention will change our lives.'

'And who knows about this progoramy?'

'Everybody.'

'So why aren't they buying it?'

'He who can't dance says the ground is full of rocks. But you and I know better than that. We dance like there is no tomorrow.'

'And you say a chippy?' she said.

'Yes.'

'Inside my body?'

'Yes.'

'Will it hurt?'

'So tiny in your neck, you won't feel a thing.'

'Like when I cut my foot on that hoe and the dokita at the clinic did me tetanus with a needo and I didn't get sick?'

'Yes, easy like a shot. You're doing this for us. For you and me and Mukasa. And your parents. I can work with no worry about data on my phone, and you can send more money to your people. It's important that you do this, Natukunda.'

'For whaty?'

'Unlimited data. It's called Bluetooth. Waves from your body will connect with my smartphone and we'll pair. You'll never need a telephone for yourself—your whole body will be a smartphone. And I'll never need to buy data bundles again. It all comes with the chip.'

'Bullytoothy for how long?'

'It lasts a lifetime', he said.

'And a man named after the rediyo told you this?'

'When you show the moon to a child, it sees only your finger. Natu, try and see the shiny moon beyond the finger.'

'Why can't you do it?' she asked, as Mukasa whimpered drowsy-eyed at her breast. She tucked her wrap around him. 'You take the chippy, Kaikara.'

'A woman is the queen of the Earth. The code needs your fertile body to work properly.'

* * *

Truth wakes him at night in a sense of another life. He feels below the surface, needs a hospital now. The glint in a glazed eye, what can he trust? The sound of breaking between them. Her eyes now close from his lie, a promise that ushered vultures. She's forgotten how to dance to his whisper. And all he knows is to fall. But he remembers everything.

* * *

Everyone was complicit in a fact that was neither fiction nor myth, but data. It did not depend on age or knowledge, just the insertion of a chip that started with an ideology and set into code. What happened after was unprecedented.

The first victim was Natukunda, in her twenties—she lived in Old Kampala. She started displaying black moods and nearly battered her toddler Mukasa to death, if her husband hadn't snatched away the ill-fortuned waif.

By nightfall of the same day, the woman was complaining of severe fatigue. She refused to eat or drink, even when a relative girl—a teenaged daughter of a cousin of a cousin of an aunt—brought the woman her favourite plate of luwombo: cassava meal steamed in banana leaves and served in groundnut sauce.

Natukunda wouldn't consume anything all through the next day. She developed a dread to be seen and spoke in undone language, dreams inside dreams. When her husband dragged her from dark pockets under the bed, in a corner of the pit latrine, under sacks in a grain store... she came out scratching at him and tearing at her neck. But she also displayed a shortness of breath.

The mental aberration when it happened exposed the woman to have forgotten her own name, that of her child and her husband's.

'Natu', said the husband. 'It's me, Kaikara.'

She blinked at him.

By the time her eyes lolled and her body shuddered, she was sobbing through tissue, blood and spit. It was too late to predict anything other than her chest would stop moving. Her pulse dimmed and then vanished, and no air came out of her nose.

Just then, glass-eyed, she gave one last shudder.

Heaving words fell from her sigh and cast swirling. They formed a line like night ink and, to anyone who could read—sadly, her husband couldn't—the words in a jumble said, 'Live, tracking, assessment, non-conformance, positioning, proof-of-concept, market, network usage volatile sad unmute hop on hop on hoponhoponhoponhopon nononononononono.'

* * *

The programmer climbed onto the roof of the penthouse in Muyenga for a full view of the moon. This suburb, famous for its hills, was the Hollywood of the diaspora. It showcased in the top ten richest neighbourhoods in the world. Looking out at the horizon, he understood it was the first time he had fished in a sea of wealth swollen with ghosts of lost dreams.

On the roof, right there between scarlet dust and a galaxy of waltzing stars, he shut his eyes from tragic memories. What happened in Old Kampala was the first of anomalies.

Najoom

Gulzar

Translated by Masooma Ali

Travelling at a speed of one lakh eighty-six thousand miles a second and continuing to do so for sixty seconds you will cover crores of miles in a minute.

Light travels at that speed. Travelling at this speed for the full three hundred and sixty-five days of a year, we'll reach a place from where our earth just cannot be seen.

Continuing the journey and maintaining the same speed for ten thousand light years, we'll arrive at a sun that has been extinguished after burning for crores of years and is about to die out completely, except for occasional eruptions, out of which flames leap up to a height of twenty to twenty-five thousand miles.

Scientific data confirms that the last time this phenomenon occurred, its radiance was observed from the Earth in 1841 and 1854 respectively.

The shape of that sun is no longer like the round sun we see every day. It has spread like ink from an overturned inkpot on a dhurrie. If you were to look through a very powerful telescope when the atmosphere is absolutely clear, you would see a spot which looks like one made by the black jamuns that Sikandar often stuffs into his shirt pocket on his way back from school.

How far away that sun is! And that sun has a name too. The name is 'Eta Carinae'.

This name was given to the sun by us. Just as the viewers from the world in outer space must have given a name to our sun.

It was the year 1841 in undivided India. The Mughal king Akbar-e-Sani had died four years ago—four years that seemed to have passed in a wink—and Zafar was now on the throne.

Editors' note: 'Najoom': stars

The poet Ibrahim Zauq was ustad to Zafar, but Zafar valued and admired the poet Ghalib greatly. And Kalloo, Ghalib's domestic servant, used to often tell Munir, 'You know, the badshah secretly sends his ghazals for corrections and modifications to my master.'

'Really?' Munir would respond with wide-eyed wonder.

'I tell you, he does! He may or may not be the badshah, but he too plays up to the famous poets. Big baskets full of mangoes are sent to the house from the royal orchards.'

Munir's face would light up like a sparkling cracker. Stars glinting in his eyes, he would tell Kalloo, 'Just you wait and see. Mirza Nausha's* star will blaze forth like a torch one day.'

Munir was a great admirer of Ghalib. However, he did not know him closely. Whenever he saw him, he just saluted him by touching his forehead with reverence.

Munir was deeply interested in astronomy. He often asked questions of the people who had knowledge about stars.

'Please tell me something, hakim saheb. I have often seen a shooting star, but why do the stars move? The pole star remains fixed in the north like God's light to give directions to the moving caravans. But there are those seven stars, the ones recognised as saptarishis by Pandit Shivnath, which are seen above the minaret of the mosque—there', he indicated the direction. 'But when I wake up in the middle of the night, I see all seven of them standing guard over my head! I get so nervous; I wonder how and when they come up like that. Wondering what they would be up to next, I fall asleep again. Early in the morning, I see them moving towards the Jamuna, in the direction of Shahdara.'

Hakim saheb explained with great patience, 'Look, Munir miyan. The sky you see rises and falls in all its totality. Imagine that you are sitting under a dome and the dome is rotating over your head. All the heavenly bodies, the sun, the moon and the stars are fixed inside the dome. They are figures which only God can read. He keeps count of them.'

---

* Ghalib

'And after Him, only you can read them, hakim saheb', Munir said happily. Hakim saheb's explanation had pleased him.

Hakim saheb answered with great humility, 'Astaghfirullah! What am I, miyan. I learn only as much as He reveals.'

'Remember the night when we saw a falling star blazing through the sky and you had said some great man had departed from the earth? Well, Badshah Akbar-e-Sani had breathed his last that day.'

'It is like this, Munir miyan. When a falling star is seen, it is a forewarning of disaster in the direction where it falls. And some famous entity dies in the direction where it has broken from. Now, we did not know that it was the star of badshah salamat but its blaze indicated that his radiant light had completed its course in the world. As a matter of fact, that star had been glimmering for several days. I had been watching it.'

'All these must be the stars of the destiny of God's creatures, then. He must have put numbers on them—some big and some small.'

'Yes, of course!'

'Do you think I too have a star among them?'

Hakim saheb paused for a moment and answered reluctantly. 'Yes. It must be there.' By now he was somewhat bored with Munir's prattle. Resting his head on the bolster, he started fanning himself with a hand fan. Instantly, Munir took it from his hand and started fanning him.

'Well, hakim saheb, Mirza Nausha's star must also be present in the sky.'

'Hmm.' Hakim saheb had placed his head on the bolster. A post-dinner indolence was already weighing down his eyes.

Munir spoke to him in a conspiratorial tone, 'Mirza Nausha is bound to become the ustad of the badshah one day. His star would then shine at the place where Zauq's is situated at present. The stars must be shifting from place to place according to people's rise in position.'

By then hakim saheb was fast asleep.

Munir spent part of each night gazing at the stars and trying to identify them.

In the same year—in 1841, that is—Munir grew restless on spotting a star which was shining brighter than the others. He arrived at hakim saheb's house at the crack of dawn and mentioned his discovery to him. Hakim saheb had not seen it as he had returned from Agra that day and had gone to bed early. Munir had mentioned the star to others, too. Some of them had said they hadn't noticed it but others said they had.

The same star arose again the next night. It was indeed brighter than the other stars. When it was spotted at the same place on the third night and the others also spoke about it, hakim saheb sat up and took note of the event. Munir was highly gratified the day hakim saheb acknowledged his greetings and asked him to sit by his side.

'Arrey, Munir miyan, you have a magnificent vision. I have heard that star of yours being talked about in the badshah's court today. The royal astrologer has declared that the ascent of this star over India is an auspicious sign. He has predicted that the fortunes of the Mughal dynasty would take a turn for the better, and glory and splendour would be restored to them.'

Munir lifted his hands in prayer and said, 'Ameen', adding 'Inshallah, there would be a change for the better in the fortune of our Mirza Ghalib, too. The first anthology of his verse is scheduled for publication next month. All these are signs of happy days to come.'

The bright star remained in the sky for a few days and then disappeared. Hoping to spot it again, Munir searched hard and waited for its return.

Several years went by. Circumstances in Delhi deteriorated. The British established their supremacy.

Munir got married in 1844. Two or three children were born to him and his wife in as many years. But he did not give up his habit of stargazing at night. He hoped to find his own star in the heavens somehow. And surely the stars of his wife and children would be located somewhere close to his own. But he searched in vain. Hakim saheb's sight had begun to weaken—he had never been one for stargazing much; now, he found it difficult to read and interpret the capers of the stars even in books.

It was in 1854 again that, one night, Munir saw a falling star streaking through the sky with a long trail of light following it. In the morning, he was on his way to hakim saheb's house to inform him of the phenomenon when he learned that Ustad Zauq had passed away. Munir was convinced that what he had seen the previous night was the star of the deceased.

He went and informed Kalloo who ran to tell his master Mirza Ghalib, who was at that moment busy tending to his half-demented brother.

Another amazing thing happened after a few days. The bright star that he had noticed thirteen years earlier in 1841 had reappeared in the sky exactly at the spot from where Zauq's star had descended from the sky. It shone as radiant as before at the same place for several nights. The same year Mirza Asadullah Khan Ghalib became Badshah Bahadur Shah Zafar's ustad and was honoured with the title of Najmuddaulah Dabir-ul-Mulk.

Munir was convinced that he had identified at least one star and he believed that his own star must be situated in the same expanse of the firmament.

Betrayal

Meenakshi Bharat

Two days ago, if someone had told him that he would be standing at The Opening, he would have laughed. There were other infinitely more pressing matters at hand! Matters like the allocation of key ministerial portfolios.

Himaryan had been reasonably sure that his credentials were solid. After all, hadn't he been trained by two of the best in the game? One, the State Minister of the country—the head of state—and the other, the Party Chief! There had never been a more powerful duo in the seventy-five-year history of the nation—the current dominant world power—the country that would steer the world from the turbulent twenty-first century into a happening twenty-second. For Himaryan, independent charge of the Public Relations Ministry had been the one single driving dream behind joining politics. And now, he was close to realising it! Who else held the key to public opinion? Who else had the power to, almost single-handedly, orchestrate the outcome of the grand political jig of this vast nation?

Himaryan was a proud citizen of a political state that had emerged from a distillation of the various political philosophies prevailing a century ago. The young nation—a mere baby in the context of the hoariness of world history—gloriously drew a demographic component from diverse ethnicities and linguistic groups that populated the globe. Indeed, reeling under the repeated assaults of violent chauvinistic divisiveness, the founding fathers had been driven by a most laudable ideology—to lay the foundation of a political entity where all found a home—regardless of the colour of skin; regardless of the language they spoke or the religion they followed. Where all would get equal opportunities to rise, and to participate in the making of the nation. That was the motto which had subsequently been given official recognition by being enshrined in the country's brand-new constitution.

These were the core ideals that had enticed Himaryan. These were the principles that continued to excite him. Little wonder that the run-up to every election, held democratically every four years, saw well-meaning individuals vying to work for the betterment of the country and the consolidation of the abiding principles of the hallowed constitution.

At least that was how it was intended! Himaryan hadn't realised that the scramble for the coveted position of Sole Charge of the PR Ministry would be so cut-throat and vicious. Out of nowhere, a cloud of intrigue had sailed in to darken the pavilion. Deafening murmurs and slicing looks assailed the fraught days and nights. Only the other day, he had bumped into AarDee, his civil services batchmate and escapade-pal of their training days.

'I must commend you for the Minister's announcement of Ry 20,000 aid to migrant families returning to their homes. Well-timed to catch the monthly unlocking of The Opening!' AarDee had observed slyly. 'Effectively scotched any possibility of a sympathy wave.' Without letting up, he had continued with his silky innuendoes, 'I must also add, that turning it into a campaign proclaiming the magnanimity of the government was a real coup. Yes, a coup! And the award for the best tableau in the New Year Parade to the Migrant Parent Tableau sealed it! Yes, sealed it!' AarDee's old habit of repeating his words now took on sinister overtones, the old batchmate bonhomie lost in his double-edged jibe.

Himaryan, never at a loss for words, fell back on their common mother tongue to diffuse the bite of the moment. 'Yes brother, circumstances beyond our control forced the decision to ask all outsiders to return. Our hearts bleed for them and... the Party has decided that The Opening will be kept open for forty-eight hours—a whole twenty-four hours more than the usual one day—to make it easier for the unfortunate souls.'

The Opening in question was a huge gate that had been installed thirty years ago in the twenty-foot-high peripheral wall, built to safeguard the country and its people. Ever since the COVID-19 epidemic of 2020, nations had escalated measures to contain health scares and invasions. Who could have thought that a virus would bring nations down—even drive them to extinction—even as it had spurred the rise of entirely new ones? Glorious nations like his own!

Countries that had continued to bravely claim that COVID-19 was just a figment of the limited human imagination had fallen to its onslaught. The near decimation of whole populations had resulted in wide-scale political re-grouping. National leaders who had tripped over their heels to welcome the corona cloud by announcing opportune lockdowns had come out looking like heroes. No longer did anyone pay attention to festering sores like plunging economies, starving farmers. And it was they who had seen the opportunity in new groupings. New alignments led to the silencing of dissent and the formation of states run by like-minded ideologues. Each had applauded the other publicly, and openly announced the kinship and embraced.

'Brothers and sisters...'

'Frères et soeurs...'

'Bhaiyon aur behenon...'

'Irmãos e irmãs...'

'Hermanos y hermanas...'

The idea was that people of all origins, all colours, all languages were welcome in this alliance. Everyone would have equal opportunity and an equal say in the running of the new ideal state. Political parties went out of their way to include people from all backgrounds and proudly used this fact to campaign and establish themselves as fair and open-minded formations.

At least, that was the publicly announced intention!

Certainly, it was the politically expedient one! As time had proved. But over the years, unbidden, people somehow ended up seeking out others who looked like themselves... people who spoke the same language, followed the same customs. It was as if they just couldn't help themselves!

So, it was natural for Himaryan to slip into their common tongue—the tongue of their hallowed ancestors—when he saw AarDee. 'Brother, you don't have to put up a front with me... We're on the same side. Only the other day, the Minister was praising you to the sky—if AarDee were to do this, he would have done it so... AarDee always knows exactly what needs to be done...' Himaryan smiled a warm smile even as doubts besieged his breast. Could it be that AarDee was also in the running for the charge of the PR Ministry?

Years ago, the PR Ministry—the popular appellation of the most important ministry in the government—had ousted the Home Ministry, the Finance Ministry and the Foreign Affairs Ministry from their important positions at the top. Public relations, always important in establishing and maintaining relations between the government and the public in a democracy, had now been accorded official recognition and status. Variously dubbed in lowbrow circles as the Ministry of Fakery or the ShamMin, and in the more intellectually endowed coteries, referred to, rather pompously, as the Ministry of Equivocation and Dissimulation, its power and standing had come to be widely perceived and accepted by the people. It was ironic that despite the implied critique in these rubrics and the widespread recognition of the work profile of the ministry, people seemed to be willing to be swayed and guided by its diktats. Or was it simply because they recognised its unbounded power? Or because they couldn't see how anyone could stand up against it? It was hardly surprising that the Sole Charge of the PR Ministry had come to be openly acknowledged as the second-most powerful individual in the country. Second only to the Minister of State!

Himaryan could see an immense opportunity for doing good with the PR handle; of taking his country to greater heights as a superpower. The geographical extent of the nation had never been greater... Though not quite as big as the Mongolian Empire of yore, it was certainly bigger than the 5,000,000-square-kilometre Mauryan Empire of the third century BCE!

For Himaryan, the journey to this point had not been easy. But lately, the signals had been quite clear. Or so Himaryan had reckoned. The Minister of State had started calling him personally to consult him about every little announcement, every little directive.

'Himaryan, do you think we need to tell the public about this...' or 'Himaryan, *how* do you think we should tell the people this...' Evidently, there were many things that had to be kept from the people and many that had to be presented to them... albeit from the government's perspective. All for their own good! All for the glory of the nation! And Himaryan, with his singular ability with words had always delivered. Bravo! The State Minister smiled his approval.

And yet, of late, there was something about the whole exercise that had started making him uneasy. He couldn't quite put a finger on why he had begun to feel that things were not quite right. Numerous niggling questions rose in his mind. What had happened to the one-world-one-nation dream? Where each and every individual was equal to the other, where each and every person could rub shoulders with his fellows with no restraint! And what about the old hallowed ideal of the world being one big happy family? Maybe that was the special task cut out for him. To restore the sanctity of the country's founding principles.

In part, these misgivings were the reasons for him standing at the foot of the twenty-foot fortified steel gate. He looked up at The Opening and looked this way and that, at the unending wall on either side. The Wall that had nudged out the Great Wall of China from the rank of a world wonder as the single longest man-made construction visible from outer space. The speed of its erection was the stuff of legends. Built over a decade with the most innovative and efficient construction technology, the Wall ran all along the country's extensive border. The completeness of the cover was unparalleled in the history of mankind. The twenty-foot height was maintained throughout the sprawling extent of the border, however inhospitable the terrain. Through mountains and desert, through valleys and over rivers, the Wall rose uncompromisingly over the landscape.

But the immediate impulse to come here was more personal. His father's devastating dying revelation had changed everything. Changed the way he looked at the world. Changed the way he looked at his own role in this world.

Up until now, like any youngster, he had written off the fuddy-duddy notions of his father. In fact, there were times when he had even felt ashamed of his father's unbecoming contentment with his mediocrity. Never having been rich or well-placed, his father was quite happy with whatever little he had, and had achieved. It was quite confounding! Himaryan was beset by a burning desire to break out. To change all that!

But now, he knew why his father felt the way he did!

'Son, I have struggled with this all *your* life… At times, I felt that it was best to let things lie. At others, that it was your right to know the truth', so saying, his father halted in his words, evidently still feeling the strain of his difficult decision. 'But now that it is time for me to go, I feel even more than ever that you *need* to know.'

His father's breathing became laboured, as his agitated words struggled to come out, 'Son, I am not your biological father. Your real father had died on the difficult trek to The Opening. From the other side. He was accompanied by his wife—your mother—and his infant son—you. With the breadwinner dead, your mother would have been turned back immediately—as per the law. When your mother came in for the interview at the check post, I was in charge. She was absolutely distraught. She was weeping and all she kept repeating was, "We were doing this only for this little one." Something made me take an instant decision. I somehow managed to get both of you to my car and I told your mother to remain hidden till I came back.'

At that moment he was racked by a bout of coughing. Himaryan automatically extended a glass of water to his father's flaking lips. His father took a sip and then waved him away. His voice had taken on a real urgency now. 'Son, believe me, it was the hope that I could give a little boy a chance in life that made me take that decision. I have never regretted it. Over the years, I have come to love you more than life… I love you, son. Forgive me for taking so long to tell you the truth but I was scared how you might take it. Scared that you might reject me.' Exhausted, his father had then slipped into a deep sleep. He never woke up.

All his life, he had paid no heed to his kind-hearted, well-meaning dad's exhortations to show more compassion to the less fortunate. Adolescent rebellion and a wanting-to-make-it-big youngster's upward-turned gaze had blinded him. It was strange that now, in the moment when his father had told him that he was not his real father, he actually felt proud to be his son! In that moment he understood that it did not matter in the least bit that they did not share the same blood. What did matter was that it was this man who had now taught him the value of humanity and kinship!

It was at that moment of realisation that he received a call from the State Minister's office telling him of the unrest at The Opening. Could Himaryan come up with an official pronouncement on this?

Himaryan said he would. But to give a comprehensive official line, he would need to go to the site to get the complete picture.

So, here he was. At The Opening.

He stood on the pavement behind the grim guard manning the barricaded check post.

He was totally unprepared for what he saw. He saw the reality that his words had been responsible for covering up… the grim reality that he himself had never been aware of.

He watched the laboured trudge of humanity through to the other side. Some wept as they moved forward. Listless children with glazed looks clutched weakly at their despairing parents' hands. Anyone who dared to break away was shouted back in line by cane-wielding guards.

How were they any different from the pre-2020, pre-realignment world? Certainly, in his world, lying and deception had been institutionalised and raised to the level of a fine political art.

Where had they gone wrong? When had they slid back? Or had they ever moved forward at all? He wondered.

The order for the closing of The Opening had been given and the mechanical doors were drawing shut slowly and noiselessly with an ominous finality.

Did he want to be on this side or that?

He had worked for this moment all his life. But now he was assailed with doubt. Did he want to take the oath? Did he want to be part of the system?

Should he attempt to turn the tables from the inside, to put his training to use?

He didn't know what lay on the other side. He didn't know whether it would be any different on the other side. But at least there were possibilities! He was willing to risk it.

He walked purposefully to The Opening and slipped to the other side, just before the door locked shut.

Fake News

Let's Talk Trojan Bee

Alex Cothren

I

There is shock and horror in the Californian almond region tonight.

—CBS Sacramento

Initial reports suggest ten dead and at least a dozen more injured.

—CNN

America's latest atrocity occurred in an idyllic, sun-dappled almond grove.

—'Mass Shooting at Waterford Nut', *The New York Times*

With police confirming the deceased shooter as 32-year-old Toby Rogen, the burning question now becomes: why?

—Fox News

Mr Rogen's social media presence suggests a disturbed individual with an unhealthy grudge against bees.

—'Waterford Nut Shooter Feared "Bee-vasion"',
The Huffington Post

II

Bees are the unsung, unpaid laborers of the American agricultural system.

—'A World without Bees', *Time*

The principal mode of pollination of many plant species is by insects. Worldwide, an estimated 400 crop species are pollinated by bees... possible crop loss in some species would be more than 90% in the absence of bees.

—'Climate Change: Impacts, Adaptation,
and Vulnerability', IPCC

Any factor that compromises honeybees' abilities to forage effectively can drive a colony into decline.

—'Death of the Bee Hive', *ScienceDirect*

Researchers at Northwestern University conducted a two-year, in situ field experiment that altered the temperature of honeybees' nests to simulate a warming climate... 35% of bees died in the first year, and 70% died in the second year.

—'Climate Change Linked to Population Decline in Honeybees', *Northwestern News*

Over the coming decades, every region of the United States is expected to experience hotter temperatures and more frequent and intense heat waves.

—'Heat Waves and Climate Change', UCS

III

Over three-quarters of remaining American honeybee colonies were wiped out last year, triggering fresh panic in the agricultural industry.

—*PBS NewsHour*

A fourth straight year of cataclysmic colony die-offs has left scientists in no doubt: climate change is killing our bees.

—'Here's Why All the Bees Are Dying', *Mother Jones*

A United States Department of Agriculture study estimated that over $50 billion a year in American harvests were threatened by the mounting toll.

—'Bee Deaths Put Crops at Risk', *The Wall Street Journal*

'Listen', she says, gesturing out to rows of vineyards sparsely dotted with anaemic, dusty grapes.

I tell her I can't hear a thing.

'Exactly.'

—'Without Bees, Napa Valley Withers on the Vine', *The Atlantic*

One shopper we spoke to rejoiced that they would no longer have to pretend almonds were a delicious snack alternative, or waste precious minutes of their day testing the softness of avocados.

—'Good News for Lovers of Wheat, Rice', *The Onion*

IV

In this region heavily reliant on almond production, hope had all but died.

—'Beemigrants Divide Rural Community', *LA Times*

Unable to source natural or industrial pollinators, the Huckleberg family knew they were left with few options to save their fifth-generation apple farm.

—'Our Mysterious Savior', *The Washington Post*

Like many others in the region, Jim and Sandy Freese were about to begin the costly but unavoidable recourse of replacing their cherry orchard with wind-pollinating wheat.

—'Miracle on the American Farm', *The New Yorker*

Haemorrhaging money, Waterford Nut had already begun employee lay-offs. Then, CEO Jerry Waterford Jr got a phone call he will never forget.

—'US Almonds Back from the Brink', *Forbes*

Suddenly, mysteriously, the bees were back.

—'What's With These Bees?', *Slate*

V

The silent flowers had come to buzzing, bumbling life.

—'Tracing the Beemigrant', *National Geographic*

Incredibly, pollinator supply is almost back to pre-crisis levels.

—'The Bees Are Back in Town', *The Economist*

It appeared that the Huckleberg farm was saved.

—'Our Mysterious Savior', *The Washington Post*

Jerry Jr shakes his head, as if still in disbelief: 'God heard our prayers.'

—'US Almonds Back from the Brink', *Forbes*

Though these bees have gathered nicknames like pollen, Sandy Freese only ever calls them one thing: 'they're our savior bees'.

—'Miracle on the American Farm', *The New Yorker*

VI

Not everyone, however, is so sure about these new saviors.

—'Beemigrants Divide Rural Community', *LA Times*

Isn't it a little unnerving how, you know, these bees just 'showed up'?

—*Fox & Friends*

'They do make me uneasy', admits Walter Cromack, whose alfalfa farm was suddenly inundated this past spring.

—'The Enigma of the "Savior Bee"', *National Review*

Once again, the mainstream media is failing to ask the important questions.

—'BUZZ-KILL: Who Are These Bees Really "Saving?"', *Breitbart*

Who do these bees work for?

—*InfoWars*

VII

They're just bees, okay? Chill. They're just bees.

—'Enough Already with These Beespiracies', *Vice*

Scientists have concluded that the 'saviour bee' is in fact *Melipona beecheii*, or the Mayan stingless bee.

—'US "Saviour Bees" are Migrants', *The Guardian*

Many people in the US would not have heard of stingless bees, as the species is not cold-tolerant and lives mainly in the tropics.

—'Stingless Bees Get Their Moment in the Sun', *Nature*

Prior to this recent migration, likely due to warming temperatures, the stingless bee's natural range was thought to be from Costa Rica to Mexico.

—'Mass Migration of *Melipona Beecheii*', *Bee World*

So climate change cooked our honeybees, and then gave us some heat-loving, Central American pollinators as recompense. Problem solved, mystery over. Right?

—'What's With These Bees?', *Slate*

VIII

Agricultural production is mysteriously booming in what some are calling 'the miracle on the American farm'.

—BBC News

In the season after the new bees arrived, the Freeses yielded their largest-ever cherry crop.

—'The Miracle on the American Farm', *The New Yorker*

The Huckleberg farm wasn't just saved—it was reborn.

—'Our Mysterious Savior', *The Washington Post*

Waterford Nuts has seen a 150% increase in profits.

—'US Almonds Back from the Brink', *Forbes*

On Sundays, the church is packed with farmers grateful for the miraculous upturn in fortune. Some, however, continue to see only the devil's handiwork.

—'Beemigrants Divide Rural Community', *LA Times*

IX

An alarming new report from the Department of Homeland Security shows a surge in the number of migrants crossing into the US illegally.

—'Illegal Border Crossings Are Up', *El Paso Times*

Record numbers of migrants are streaming into the United States, overwhelming border agents and leaving holding cells dangerously overcrowded.

—'Crisis at the Border', *The Arizona Republic*

Before this latest surge, undocumented immigration had previously been in steep decline for years—a result of stricter enforcement and the rise of robotic labor.

—'Illegal Immigration to the US is Rising Again', *Houston Chronicle*

Officials are scrambling to explain this sudden and irrepressible immigration surge.

—'In Washington, Contesting Theories on Immigration Increase', *Politico*

Some have begun to wonder: is it the bees?

—'Enough Already with These Beespiracies', *Vice*

X

Locals have a nickname for the opportunistic, undocumented workers who are suddenly everywhere: 'beemigrants'.

—'Beemigrants Divide Rural Community', *LA Times*

It does appear that many of those arriving illegally find work in the burgeoning fields and orchards of the 'savior bee'.

—'Are Bees Key to Immigrant Surge?', *Newsweek*

Productivity just happens to be booming in one of the few areas robotics is yet to comprehensively figure out: labor-intensive and difficult-to-pick crops like cherries, apples, and almonds.

—'Robotics' Achilles Heel is Beemigrants' Boon', *Wired*

One of the few areas still reliant on low-skilled foreign workers is therefore also one of the fastest growing.

—'New Trends in Illegal Immigration', Pew Research Centre

'We're sure this is all just an innocent coincidence.'

—'Internet Calls for Calm, Common Sense on Beemigrant Issue', *The Onion*

XI

Let's talk 'Trojan Bee'.

—*InfoWars*

The open-border craving globalists, through multinationals like Monsanto and Bayer, dramatically and deliberately reduced the US honeybee population via neonicotinoids, thus goading the Mainstream Media into 'bee-pocalypse' hysteria.

—'Globalist Pesticides Were behind Massive Honeybee Die-off', *ZeroHedge*

Then came the secret release of a genetically modified bee, one lab-designed to radically boost the productivity of certain crops reliant on cheap foreign labor.

—'The Dark Agenda of the Trojan Bee', *Alt-Market*

Distracted by the 'gift' of this 'savior', and the 'endangered' crops it has supposedly saved, the American public was primed to accept the filthy hordes crossing in the bees' wake.

—'The Trojan Takeover Has Bee-gun', *Daily Stormer*

With the borders now successfully overrun by illegal aliens, the loony left and the globalist MSM cabal are attempting to deflect via their favorite manufactured culprit: climate change.

—'BUZZ-KILL: Who Are These Bees Really "Saving?"', *Breitbart*

XII

Scientists have determined that climate change, and not the so-called 'savior bee', is the main cause of our boosted crop yields.

—MSNBC

Whereas most tropical regions have experienced production losses due to rising temperatures, production in temperate regions is benefitting from the warmer climate and longer growing seasons.

—'UN Report Identifies Where Global Harvests Have Risen', Centre for American Progress

An atmosphere with more CO_2 boosts crop yield in the short term via increased rates of photosynthesis.

—'How Climate Change Actually Helps Some Farmers', *Scientific American*

Fleeing the devastating heat and drought of their natural habitats, *Melipona beecheii* arrived at a fecund region desperate for pollinators.

—'Our Opportunistic "Saviors"', *ThinkProgress*

These 'refubees' moved north because our farmland could save *them*, not vice versa. And they're not alone.

—'Savior Bee or Refubee?', *The Huffington Post*

XIII

Like the bees before them, there is a simple reason migrants—or 'beemigrants'—are travelling north en masse: desperation.

—'The Truth about These "Beemigrants"', *Mother Jones*

In the settlement of Plan del Jocote, Chiquimula, Gloria Diaz's crops didn't produce a single grain of corn.

—'Changing Climate Is behind Migration Surge', *The Guardian*

It's the height of monsoon season in Mexico, but in the village of Zapopan, the rains came months too late, then stopped altogether.

—'Linkages among Climate Change, Crop Yields and Mexican Migration', *PNAS*

After a season of merciless drought, and with his starving family surviving only on the dwindling mantiocas they could find in the surrounding scrubland, Juan Uribe Francisco was left with no other choice but to head north.

—'Tracing the Beemigrant', *National Geographic*

There is no mystery here, no conspiracy. There are just desperate people looking for our help at the exact same moment we need theirs.

—'Let's Squash the "Trojan Bee"', *San Francisco Chronicle*

XIV

A shortage of migrant workers is resulting in lost crops in California.

—'Californian Crops Rot due to Immigrant Farmworker Shortage', *Fortune*

Despite the recent migration surge, farmers with record yields are still struggling to get enough hands on board, and Americans appear to have no interest in picking fruit.

—'Can Immigration Reform Fix the Agricultural Job Shortage?', *The Wall Street Journal*

United States agriculture cannot afford to waste this opportunity. If American workers are unwillingly to help, you need to increase our migrant workforce ASAP.

—Jerry Waterford Jr, Testimony to Senate Judiciary Subcommittee on Border Security and Immigration

Under pressure from the agricultural lobby and the public outcry over rotting crops, Congress passed a historic law today that drastically simplifies the H2A farmworker visa process, essentially giving instant employment to the thousands of asylum seekers detained along our southern border.

—'Congress Passes "Farmworker Shortage" Bill', *RealClearPolitics*

Predictably, not everyone is pleased.

—'The Alt-Right Has Absolutely Flipped Its Lid over This New Farmworker Law', *BuzzFeed*

XV

Welp, the puppet cucks in Congress just bent America over and lubed her up.

—Gab

No one can still credibly claim that the 'Trojan Bee' is a conspiracy theory. It's not even a *theory* anymore—it's an event happening before our very eyes.

—YouTube

We're screwed. Time to start learning Spanish, amigos.

—4chan

Good news: the upcoming midterms are an opportunity to protest this BS.
Bad news: who the f ya gonna vote 4?????

—Twitter

Riding the wave of anger over recent visa reform, anti-immigrant third-party candidates are popping up all over the country.

—'Midterms Rocked by Angry New Party', *The Nation*

XVI

This new political force in America is vehemently anti-immigrant and, yes, anti-bees.

—'What Exactly Does the Bread Party Want?', *Salon*

A dark thread of conspiracy weaves through their political views. In their world, the recent H2A bill is proof of a 'globalist' conspiracy to promote immigrant anarchy via boosted agriculture yields.

—'Introducing (sigh) the "Bread Party"', *The New Republic*

#3: Demand that all genetically modified Anthophilas be destroyed, and that those operating the labs face criminal punishment.

—Shut the Gates, Purge the Fields: A Bread Party Manifesto

Their unhinged and hyperbolic manifesto explains that 'bread' represents 'but one of the many wholesome products Americans can still enjoy once our immigrant infestation has been purged'.

—'Explaining the Dumbest Name in Politics', *Vox*

Aside from believing in far-fetched conspiracy theories, supporters also adhere to a boycott on all food products relying on bees.

—'Inside the Strange World of the Bread Party', *Vogue*

XVII

Patriot-purge complete: strawberries, almonds, apples, blueberries, all night-night down the garbage disposal.

—r/bread_party

[Safeway employees sniffing in fruit section, looking confused]
Them: did someone piss on these melons?
Me: ☺
#BPRise

—Twitter

This is the fourth Missoula fruit store this week to be tagged with swastikas.

—*KPAX Nightly News*

What do we eat? Bread! What do we grow? Wheat!

—Bread Party rally, Mobile, Alabama

'We are officially redundant.'

—'Every Satirist Everywhere Retires', *The Onion*

XVIII

Brad Hardigan (R) 59%, Sally Litchfield (D) 31%, Elijah Mason (B) 10%

—Midterm results, Mobile County, Alabama

Election night was a resounding disapprobation of this new party's toxic worldview.

—'Bread Party Fails to Rise', *The New York Times Magazine*

Despite encouraging returns in some southern states, their cocktail of nativist fury and tinfoil gobbledegook is unlikely to ever tempt mainstream voters.

—'Bread Party Stuck with Heel of Midterm Loaf', *FiveThirtyEight*

They may have been roundly defeated, but those writing off the Bread Party do so at their own peril.

—'Still Plenty of Slices Left for Bread Party', *The Weekly Standard*

Worryingly, their poor election results seem to have only deepened their conspiratorial tendencies.

—'Bread Party Hardens Conspiracy Crust', *The Economist*

XIX

Across the country, Bread Party candidates are refusing to concede, claiming electoral fraud.

—'Bread Party Seeks Midterm Recount', NPR

Mississippi candidate Timothy McKee, who lost in the state's fourth congressional district, today said that 'illegals voted early and they voted often'.

—'Bread Party: Illegal Immigrants Swayed Election', *The Clarion-Ledger*

A Bread Party demonstration in Charleston turned violent today, as supporters brawled with Antifa protestors outside the West Virginia State Capitol building.

—*WDVM News*

They are so far down the road of this ridiculous conspiracy that it is hard to say what will happen when reality hits.

—'The Bread Party Has Nowhere to Go', *The American Prospect*

Citing no evidence to support claims of widespread voter fraud, the voting integrity commission today rejected the possibility of special recounts.

—'Report: No "Significant" Voting Fraud in Midterms', Bloomberg

XX

Juan Uribe Francisco, 30; Carlos Gomez Garcia, 31; Julio Ernesto Acuna Garcia, 23; Javier Hernandez, 25; Enrique Hernandez Lopez Obrador, 28; Nelson Roberto Espinal Matamoros, 34; Anabell Pineda, 26; Joaquin Sabina, 37; Jose Luis Tepeu, 22; Andres Luis Videgaray, 30.

—'These Are the Victims of the Waterford Nut Shooting', *People*

Witnesses say that Mr Rogen was shooting at workers and bees alike.

—'Waterford Nut Shooter Feared "Bee-vasion"', *The Huffington Post*

He was a registered Bread Party member, and his posts on Facebook, Twitter, and Gab echoed alt-right conspiracies such as the 'trojan bee'.

—'Did the Bread Party Cause the Waterford Nut Shooting?', *Daily Kos*

In a final, chilling post he claimed that 'beelegals' would pay for 'stealing the election'.

—'The Last Days of the Waterford Nut Shooter', *USA Today*

One can only pray that this is a turning point, and that the extreme fringes of our political spectrum learn to tone down their rhetoric.

—'The Tragic Lesson of the "Trojan Bee"', *The New Yorker*

XXI

Two words: false flag.

—*InfoWars*

A guy walks into a busy orchard with an AK-17 and only kills eight people? #WaterfordNot

—Twitter

Sure, it's not at all suspicious that his social media postings parrot 'trojan bee' theories verbatim.

—'The Details of That Almond Shooting Are... Weird', *The Daily Wire*

Notice how the 'victims' are all illegals no one can trace?

—r/bread_party

'A false flag is always an attempt by those in power to trick the public into fearing something. In this case: us.'

—'Bread Party Calls "False Flag" on Waterford Nut Shooting', *Gateway Pundit*

XXII

In a rare display of unanimity, Congress passed legislation today effectively barring the Bread Party from American politics.

—'Congress Bans Controversial Party', *Politico*

The Bread Party Control Act 'criminalizes membership in, or support for the party, and defines evidence to be considered by a jury in determining participation in the activities, actions, objectives, or purposes of said party'.

—'The Bread Party is Cooked', *The Daily Beast*

The new legislation is based on the Communist Control Act of 1954.

—'Yes, There Is Precedence for Kicking Out a Political Party', *Slate*

While some—in the wake of the Waterford Nut Shooting—see necessary action, others fret that extreme measures could have adverse consequences.

—'Out of the Frying Pan, into the Oven?', *The Economist*

Lock and load.

—r/bread_party

XXIII

There is shock and horror in the Michigan blueberry region tonight.

—NBC Detroit

Mourners have lit candles and placed wreaths outside of this family-owned alfalfa farm.

—CBS Des Moines

A once-peaceful cherry orchard is now a ghastly crime scene.

—NBC Portland

Napa Valley is stunned by this latest outbreak of violence, the tenth to occur across the country this week alone.

—Fox Oakland

Miguel Angel Gonzalo, 27; Tom Huckleberg, 47; Jill Huckleberg, 42; Janice Huckleberg, 13; Tom Huckleberg Jr, 6; Gabriel Latorre, 29; Paulo Torreria, 35; Francisco Javier Rodriguez-Rodriguez, 20; Alejandro Ricardo Sanchez, 34.

—'These Are the Victims of the Huckleberg Apple Shooting', *People*

XXIV

Is this really how America falls apart? Over *bees*?

—'Are We at War?', *Chicago Tribune*

This time, the terrorists are us.

—'Nothing to Fear but Fear Ourselves', *The Atlantic*

A preposterous conspiracy theory—about bees no less—has exposed the fault lines of our tenuous Union.

—'The Stupid War We've Long Had Coming', *Intelligencer*

The more vehement the denials of the 'trojan bee', the more violent the response seems to be.

—'This War Will Not be Won by Logic', ProPublica

By the conflict's end, the death toll stood at near ten thousand humans as well as countless numbers of bees.

—'From Pizzagate to the Trojan Bee:
Ten Conspiracy Theories That Turned Deadly', *Listverse*

Party Lights

Tony Birch

Pete had often pondered the range of possibilities contributing to his memory loss. Each of them was fanciful, and a long way from the truth. Any reputable doctor or friend, even *the man in the street*, knew enough about the limits of the human body to conclude that a decade-long habit of hammering a cocktail of drugs had left holes in Pete's brain. He'd shot, snorted and smoked every substance on the market. As a result, he sometimes had trouble remembering his birthdate and telephone number. On one occasion, after a week of binging underground at an abandoned opal mine, he not only forgot his name but the face he saw in the mirror. On a bad day, nobody was more alien to Pete than Pete.

He had no real friends, having been abandoned on account of repeated transgressions. He did have an acquaintance of sorts, a horse trainer, small-time dealer and fellow drug user, Hester Nixon, who'd injected more ketamine into his body than the gelding he'd trained, Good Luck Grant, to a first place at the midweek meeting in Bourke a year back. The horse had overjuiced on Special K and continued running over the finish line, despite all attempts to pull him up. Good Luck Grant didn't stop until he'd thrown the jockey and run into a nearby swamp. The racetrack steward was no doubt suspicious. The horse was tested, the drug detected and Hester lost his trainer's licence.

'What are you going to do about it?' Pete asked, when Hester told him the story.

'Do? Nothing I can do, except maybe change the name of the pony to No Luck Fucking Grant. That's what I'll do.'

'It might work', Pete laughed, 'unless they twig that it's the same horse?'

Hester's drug business was no more successful than his horse-racing venture. He downed or gave away more drugs than he sold. While Pete was no admirer of Hester's business sense, he was in awe of the man's constitution. Hester had the ability to load his body with chemicals all night and surface the next day sharp as a tack. Hester also had a remarkable capacity for storing information. In high school he'd earned the nickname *Rain Man* after displaying the unique ability to speed-read the telephone book and subsequently recall every name, address and number. He'd made decent pocket money with the act, fleecing tourists passing briefly through town to visit its single attraction, The Giant Spanner. *Banjanna*—a bullet-riddled sign on the edge of town read—*Home of The Giant Spanner.*

Pete purchased his daily dose from Hester, who bought his own supply of drugs from a rig driver who went by the uninventive name of Convoy. He pulled in regularly at the truck-stop cafe on the edge of town for 'fuel, a feed and a fuck' before beginning the long-haul desert crossing. Convoy's risk was minimal. He had one customer in each town, while those he did business with, dealers such as Hester, had a clientele of misfits, souped-up FIFOs and scab-faced teenagers to deal with.

Pete, not quite the entrepreneur himself, had once attempted to break into the trade, setting up a deal with Convoy without Hester's knowledge. His plan was to introduce drugs to the blackfella outstations and sell direct to the Vietnam veterans scattered across old mining leases in the nearby hills. The vets tended to surface in town once a month to stock up on food, drugs and dynamite, and they bought their gear from Hester. Pete would cut Hester out by taking the product on the road, delivering to the customers' doorsteps.

This entry into venture capitalism quickly fell apart. In a small town like Banjanna there were no secrets. The news quickly got to one of the blackfella head-men, Frederick Moss. Sadly, for Pete, Frederick was a man who knew the law of the street just as well as he did the *lore* of the community he took care of. Frederick came hunting Pete and found him dozing under the old blue gum out front of the weighbridge one Sunday morning. He leaned over Pete, shook him gently by the shoulder and whispered a word in his ear. Before Pete could rouse himself Frederick was laying into him with a lump of wood. Afterwards, bloodied, bruised and unable to breathe on account of several broken ribs, Pete lay on his back, sucking for air and moaning in pain. Frederick, his skin as black as coal, spoke in a deep voice. The words were eerily transmitted across the sky from one end of town to the other. 'Bring ya poison near my young ones', he cautioned, 'and I will strip ya of skin, smoke ya head and eat ya fucken kidney fat—just for beginnings.'

Pete dropped the idea for his drug business that same morning and decided to stick to what he knew best, getting as stoned as Uluru anytime he got the chance.

Pete was sitting at a table under an umbrella out front of the truck-stop one afternoon, studying a glass of water, when Hester asked if he would like to invest in a croquet lawn for the town.

'I'm giving you an early option, Pete. This could bring big dollars into town. We've got nothing here.'

'Course we do. What about The Spanner?'

'The Spanner can go fuck itself. It's an embarrassment.'

'It's no such thing. Just now, on my way here, I saw a busload of Chinese people. Or Japanese people. They were heading out to see The Spanner. Taking photographs. They love it. You know, pineapples, koalas. All that big stuff.'

'Maybe they do. But it brings fuck-all money to town. They spend five minutes taking photographs on them *selfish* sticks and then they piss off. They don't buy nothing. What the fuck was the Council thinking when they had The Spanner put in on the edge of town? The worst decision we ever made. They should have stuck it smack in the centre. We could've parked an ice-cream van across from it and made a killing.'

'Why do you care, Hes? You've got your own business.'

'I care because I'm thinking of running for Council myself one day. People need to see that I have initiative.'

'And a croquet lawn is your way of showing it? Fuck me.'

'I'd bet the viability of a croquet lawn against The Spanner any day of the week.'

Charlie Jackson, the Councillor responsible for the planning decision at the time The Giant Spanner was being voted on, and also the current mayor, was sitting two tables across from Pete and Hester and heard every word Hester said. Before going into politics, Charlie had been unpopular, building what he spruiked as *the largest factory pig farm east of the state border*. He put small farms out of business overnight. Charlie waved at Pete and Hester and smiled with genuine pleasantness. There was little that offended the man. During the election campaign he'd promised *a major new attraction to revitalise this town*. Posters of his smiling face and auburn toupee had been wallpapered on every street. Within twenty-four hours the posters had been defaced with a crudely painted red penis. One of Jackson's cronies, spotting an offending dick on a poster outside the railway station, ran into Charlie's office screaming, *We gotta take them down!*

Charlie wouldn't hear of it. *Democracy in action*, he called the act of vandalism when talking to the sole reporter of the local newspaper the following morning. Alongside the planned construction of The Giant Spanner, Charlie turned the slogan into his election platform.

The decision was ridiculed and Charlie was endlessly mocked behind his back. He was called an idiot and a dickhead. But what few people understood about Charlie Jackson was that he was a political genius. The offending posters became a key talking point of the campaign. They remained in place and Charlie made speeches repeating the words *democracy*, *democracy*, *democracy*, over and over.

While few in town cared for the concept of democracy, suspiciously labelling it a big-city invention, Charlie had somehow managed to reinvent himself as *a man of the people* and was never more popular. He killed the election. The following night he had police block the main street, had the posters torn down and organised a bonfire at the main intersection. Charlie quickly reverted to type, ending his victory speech with an ambit threat: 'If the fuckers responsible for this shit don't think I'll find you, you're wrong. And when I do, the arm you used to paint the offending organ with shall be ripped from its shoulder socket and fed to my pigs.'

What would become Hester's final purchase from Convoy led to his downfall. He and Convoy met in the Ladies toilet at the truck-stop. Hester rattled off a list of goodies he was after, to which Convoy replied *Yeah, got it, got it*, without listening to a word of what was said. Hester handed Convoy a roll of notes and received a green supermarket bag in return. As was their usual method of exchange, Hester waited in the toilet until Convoy had jumped into his rig and driven onto the highway. Hester sat on the toilet, reached into the bag and retrieved a solid pouch of weed. He opened it, stuck his nose inside and drew in the scent. He then plucked a bud and rubbed it between his thumb and fingers. The quality wasn't great and marijuana was well out of fashion in the district but once he repackaged it, he'd be able to sell it on to the young kids and ageing hippies. Hester continued to rummage through the range of lollies in the supermarket bag. He tipped the contents out of the bag and looked down at the sachets and bottles of pills of various colours, none of which were labelled. Most of the drugs looked unfamiliar. Convoy had ripped him off. Hester was able to identify no more than two slim bags of coke and what he guessed were ecstasy, on account of the ! stamped on one side of each tablet. The remaining contents of the showbag were a mystery.

Hester dropped a couple of the tablets and walked to his van at the caravan park—*Little Miami*. Sitting in the van, sniffing one of the bags of coke, Hester mulled over how to best move the unidentifiable drugs. It took two further snorts of coke and another tablet for him to realise a solution. He opened several cupboards until he found a large wooden bowl. He then poured the contents of each pill bottle into the bowl, mixed them together, and beat them with the handle of a screwdriver until he'd ground the pills to a fine powder. He added the remaining bag of coke, kept a sachet of what he believed were the ecstasy tablets for himself, and mixed the concoction together.

It was hard work. By the time he'd finished Hester's shirt was drenched in sweat. He ran his fingers through the pale coloured powder, speckled with ruby-red grains. As he moved the bowl to the kitchen sink he noticed that the red crystals sparkled and came to life. The drug took on a hallucinatory quality without him having sampled it. Hester's heart raced with excitement, convinced that he was onto something big. He quickly calculated that after cutting the powder further, he could produce around a hundred deals. The product would need to be sampled, not for precautionary reasons, but in order to *fashion the narrative*, a few of the many business buzzwords he'd picked up after watching *The New Entrepreneurs* on cable TV. The young presenter of the program, who'd become a millionaire by the time she was twenty-one, apparently selling heated slippers online, was forever reminding viewers about the secret of her success. 'Whenever you have plans to put a new product in the marketplace, it is vital that you also produce a narrative and eye-catching branding to seduce the buyer.'

Hester emptied the contents of the bowl into a plastic bag, sealed it with an elastic band and searched the van for his mobile phone, without success. He left the van and walked the pathway separating two rows of caravans. A boy on a pushbike rode towards him. Hester had seen the kid around the park. He never seemed to be at school and wore a pair of permanently blackened eyes. Each time they were on the verge of fading, fresh swelling and bruising appeared. The boy rode past Hester, turned and pedalled alongside him.

'You got something for me?' he asked.

Hester walked a little quicker. 'Fuck off, runt.'

'Fuck off yourself. You got any drugs?'

'I don't know what you're talking about.'

'You do so. And if you don't give me some I'll call the cops.'

Hester stopped on the roadway and grabbed the handlebars of the bike.

'You go to the police, retard. You know what they'll do? Your family will be put in a cage and paraded around the town, you fucken hillbillies. Piss off.'

Hester yanked the handlebars of the bike, a little too hard, and the boy fell off. He lay on his side and cried. Hester didn't want to attract the attention of the kid's family. They may have been dirt poor but they could fight like bulls. He helped him to his feet.

'I'm sorry, kid. It was an accident.'

He brushed dirt from the boy's T-shirt, reached into his side pocket and pulled out the sachet of ecstasy tablets.

'Hold out your hand', he said, and poured half a dozen tablets into the boy's palm. 'There you are. Now, don't take them all at once. And maybe stay off the pushbike. On the roads, at least.'

The boy looked down at the tablets in his hand and smiled. 'Ta.' He swallowed one, jumped on his bike, screamed 'Whoop! Whoop!' and rode away. Hester walked to the front gate of the park, stepped into the public telephone box and made a call.

'What?' Pete shouted when he picked up the phone. He sounded like a man who'd been rudely interrupted from a matter of great importance.

'Meet me out by The Spanner', Hester said.

'Why?' Pete shouted again.

'Cause I have something for you.'

'What?'

'A treat', Hester giggled. 'A real treat.'

The Giant Spanner, stretching towards the clear afternoon sky, was secured behind a three-metre-high fence topped with razor-wire. It was guarded by a CCTV camera, which may or may not have been in working order. The Council had deemed the security a necessary defence of the landmark tool following repeated acts of vandalism, including a graffiti tag identical to the penis that had desecrated the face of the would-be mayor. When Hester arrived, Pete was sitting in the red dirt, resting his back against the wire fence. Hester strode across to him and dropped the bag of powder at Pete's feet, then looked up and glared into the warm ball of sun. The head of The Giant Spanner resembled a prehistoric monster.

'Where's my treat?' Pete shouted. 'You got nothing, you fucking liar.'

Hester bent down, picked up the bag and held it by the handles, slowly swinging it from side to side like the pendulum of a grandfather clock. 'I do have it. And it's a fucken wonder.'

Pete licked his lips and reached for the bag. Hester stepped away from him. 'Not so quick. Let me show you what I've got.'

He took a dirty handkerchief from his pocket, unfolded it and laid it in the dirt. He untied the supermarket bag, reached in with his fingers and tipped a small mound of powder in the middle of the cloth. It glowed and sparkled in the sunlight. Pete's eyes lit up.

'What is it, Hes? It looks… alive.'

'What it will be, very soon, is the newest product on the market.'

'What do they call it?'

'Doesn't have a name. That's how new it is. I'm going to break it down and sell it myself. I have to come up with a product description. Something that will stick. You have any ideas?'

Pete moved closer to the handkerchief.

'Look at the way it's winking at us. Remember the old Angel Dust? Now that was a drug', he momentarily reminisced. 'Maybe you could call it Fairy Dust. Something like that. You know, because of the way it's sparkling.'

'Nah. I want something more original than that.'

Hester stared into the glowing powder. He waved his open palm over it and felt a sense of warmth on his fingertips.

'I know. *Party Lights*. What do you think?'

'*Party Lights*. Yeah. I like it. What's it do for ya?'

'You're about to find out. Pinch yourself a decent snort, Pete. It's on the house. Get it right up there in the membranes and we'll see if you go off.'

Pete hesitated. 'Do you think it's safe?'

'I hope not', Hester grinned. 'We'll see how close you can get to the sun without burning up.'

No sooner had Pete shot a pinch of the powder up his nostril than his eyes lit up. They changed colour from bright yellow, to red, to deep blue. His body shook for several seconds and relaxed. He fixed a dreamy smile on Hester.

'What's it like?' Hester asked. 'Is it good gear, Pete? Is it good?'

'I've found it. I've found it', Pete babbled.

Hester grabbed Pete by the shoulders and shook him lightly. 'Found what?'

'The world', he smiled lazily. 'I found the world. The beautiful world.'

Pete looked happier than Hester had ever seen him. His face radiated joy. Hester was so excited he dropped to his knees, scooped a handful of powder out of the bag and buried his face in it, sniffing and snorting like one of the mayor's hungry pigs at a trough of feed. He lurched forward and his face slammed into the red dirt. He could hear Pete calling his name but was unable to move. He rolled onto his side and slowly opened his eyes. He smiled at Pete, who was hovering above him with a demented grin. Pete offered a helping hand. 'Come on, Hes. We're off.'

'Where to?'

'I haven't worked it out, but we have to go.' He pointed along the highway. 'Out there. It's out there. The world.'

Hester had difficulty hearing what Pete was saying on account of the brass band playing in his head. They decided on a second snort each before venturing on their way. Pete took Hester by the hand, like a gentle father guiding an anxious son. Some way down the road, Hester looked back over his shoulder and saw a large hole in the ground, where The Giant Spanner should have been wedged into the earth. It was gone. He looked to Pete for an explanation, but Pete was busy, head tilted back, gazing into the sky and admiring the cotton clouds meeting the glow of a setting sun.

The brass band began playing the first bars of the national anthem. Hester shook his head violently from side to side in an attempt to free himself of it.

'I'm no fucken patriot', he shouted at Pete.

'What?' Pete shouted back.

'Forget it.'

Unable to dislodge the tune, Hester had no choice but to begin marching along the highway towards the desert. Pete couldn't hear the music at all, but fell into step with his friend.

Up ahead they could see a yellow front-end loader working alongside a large wooden house. The windows of the house were shattered and the timber boards were splashed with graffiti. The loader moved backwards and forwards gouging buckets of earth out of the ground. The hole was around ten metres deep and twice as wide.

As they marched closer, Hester noticed the driver of the loader possessed a remarkably rich head of silver hair. The man sat watching as they goose-stepped closer. Hester stopped and stared into the hole. Pete ignored the hole completely. Instead, he thrust an arm in the air, as if trying to grasp the final rays of the setting sun in his hand. The driver killed the loader's engine and jumped down, standing over the hole and admiring his work.

'Hey', Pete called to him, 'you dug a big hole.'

'I did', the man nodded, appreciatively.

'Hey', Hester called out. 'Have you seen a giant spanner come by this way?'

'I did, indeed.' The driver pointed west. 'It was headed that way. Flying low and fast into the sun.'

Pete was having trouble concentrating. He wandered around the edge of the hole to where the driver began rolling himself a cigarette.

The driver offered his hand. 'Jerry.'

Pete shook Jerry's hand. He couldn't remember his own name but was happy to introduce Hester, who trailed behind. Hester also shook Jerry's hand.

'For what purpose have you dug this hole?' Hester asked.

Jerry was not a man to offer a word more than he needed to. 'For filling it in.'

'With what?' Pete asked. 'The dirt you just took out of it?' He giggled.

Hester thought the comment worthy of a laugh and chuckled. Jerry took the question more seriously. 'You would be correct. Eventually most of the dirt will be returned to the hole.' He pointed in the general direction of the old house. 'First off, I'll be pushing this place into the hole and then I'll bury it.'

'You're going to bury a house?' Hester said. 'Why would you do that, Jerry?'

'Most of all because it's cheap and quick', Jerry answered. 'I get paid to demolish and remove derelict buildings from sites. One time

I used to cart these houses away on the back of a truck, find a tip that would take them and pay a large fee. One day I was looking at an old barn I was about to take down, and this idea came to me. What do they call them? Light bulbs or something?'

Hester looked across at Pete and shrugged.

'I think it must be something like that. A light bulb', Pete offered.

'You boys want to watch me go to work? Show you how efficient the process is?'

Hester wasn't sure if he wanted to see a house buried in the ground, but thought it would be rude not to show interest in Jerry's enthusiasm for his work. 'Yeah, we'd like to see that, Jerry. Wouldn't we, Pete?'

Pete had lost interest in Hester, Jerry, the house and the hole in the ground. He returned his attention to the setting sun.

Jerry hopped into the saddle of the front-end loader and drove off, rumbling across the ground, the motor spewing dirty smoke as it disappeared behind the house. Moments later the sound of breaking glass and splintering timber filled the sky. Hester watched in morbid fascination as the house tilted forward, breaking free of its rotting foundations. The sides of the house opened up, leaving the body clinging to the loader. It tumbled over the edge of the hole, rolled onto its roof and crashed into the pit, sending a cloud of red dust into the air. Hester covered his mouth and coughed. The loader mopped up the remains of the house, pushing ends of timber, glass and broken roof tiles into the ditch. Jerry filled the bucket of the loader with dirt and started filling in the hole, repeating the process until the house had disappeared. He then used the empty bucket to level and flatten the earth above the buried house. Within minutes there was little evidence the house had existed at all except for the red-gum footings poking out of the earth, resembling a set of rotting teeth.

Hester looked down at the disturbed patch of ground, mesmerised by what he'd witnessed. Jerry walked across to him. 'I must be on my way, son.'

'Where you heading?' Hester asked.

Jerry looked across the flat horizon. 'For a man in my position, the work never ceases. I'm about to head to another house, another hole in the ground. What's going on with your friend here?' he asked. 'He seems to be out of sorts?'

Pete had been hypnotised by the late afternoon sun. He stood still as a statue, marvelling at the sky and the streaks of colour shooting low on the horizon.

'Don't worry about Pete. He's always been curious.'

Jerry again shook Hester's hand. 'I'll be on my way.'

He jumped into the loader and drove onto the highway. Hester rested on his haunches and watched as the lights of the loader gradually disappeared into the looming darkness.

'You ever see anything like that before?' Hester asked Pete.

Pete scratched his head. 'Not sure. I can't say, Hes.'

'Can't say? I'd never forget it, if I'd seen something like that before, a man burying a whole house.'

'Well, Hes. You don't possess the skill set that I do. I can forget most things when I put my mind to it.'

Pete yawned. He suddenly felt very tired. He lay in the dirt alongside Hester. Within minutes he was asleep. He did not wake until early the next morning. Hester was asleep beside him, face down in the dirt. Pete nudged him in the ribs. Hester groaned and lifted his head. His body was covered in fine red dirt. He sat up and looked around. 'Where are we?' he asked.

'On the side of a road, I'm guessing.'

Hester got to his feet and dusted himself down. 'There was something here, wasn't there, Pete?'

'There's always something some place. Which way's town, you reckon?'

Hester pointed east and then west. 'Could be that way. Or maybe that way. I'm heading this way. West. You coming?'

'Not sure yet.'

'Well, I'll see you when you make up your mind.'

Pete watched as Hester walked out along the highway, tracing his own long shadow. He thought about following but had failed to decide by the time Hester had vanished into the distance. He walked across to a circle of ground and dropped to his knees. For reasons he would never be able to comprehend, Pete started digging with both hands.

Threadbare

Devika Brendon

This is a story of bloodlines and textiles. It's someone else's story, not mine. But that doesn't diminish its significance. Please listen well. There are parts that have been amplified and augmented, I admit. But in the deep weave of it, the truth resides.

Like many of us, I've lived a cocooned life, cushioned and bolstered by comforting narratives. Like all immigrants, I've been cut off from source. But, embedded in my being, there are bloodlines which tell me where I truly belong. My quest is to find them. Far flung as we all are, we are, each of us, slowly returning to our roots.

And the other thing I need to tell you is that I'm a girl. Life's more complex for us. It's incorrect to think of Asia as a wholly patriarchal society. Because, even though women are oppressed and exploited throughout the span of the wide brown lands, there are subtle matriarchal traditions which endure. And not just when it comes to marriage-making and fixing the children up with suitable boys and girls.

One of the best things about Asia is also, paradoxically, one of its most damaging aspects, if it is abused, as it often is: the extended family structure. A psychiatrist trained in Britain in the fifties, and married to my maternal aunt, once described the extended families of Asia as being 'enmeshed'. Indeed, there are myriad sticky ties evident between South Asian people, which are formed by duty, familial obligation, escutcheon, coercion and emotional leverage. 'These operate to retard and arrest the process of individuation', said my uncle, smoking at the dinner table, against my—then—as yet unexpressed wishes.

So people like us stay with their families and live in a compound, in close proximity to our immediate ancestors, long after our western counterparts have moved out into apartments and share houses, as students. Home comforts are one thing, but many people's personal independence never develops. They never know the satisfaction of their own sovereignty.

The mother of a man I almost married once observed that Indian people easily express a lot of sentiment, but not often real emotion. I think we'd been to see *Monsoon Wedding*, for context—but it was a comment I will always remember. At that time, I was sleeping on a mattress on the floor, telling myself it was better for my health.

Someone my cousin was close to had a marriage that was arranged, several years ago. It looked right on paper, and from the outside, he told me recently. The family lineages and the astrological charts had (with a little manoeuvring) been aligned. But no one concerned in making the arrangements had done their due diligence on a deeper level. Over the years, as the threads of the covering materials wore thin, the true incompatibilities of the not-so-happy couple inevitably showed through.

I heard from my cousin that, in the last few years of this union, the wife had kept up appearances by renting another apartment in the same building, but on another floor. She said she needed more space where she could have her work meetings, but in actual fact she and their daughter were living in the rented apartment. Her husband, whose parents owned the apartment she officially lived in with the man she had married, was marooned in that lower level, air-conditioned marble-floored box, with his meals sent to him. When the in-laws came to visit, the whole family had meals in the official apartment, at the rosewood table imported from Singapore, so no one knew how long the actual deception and dereliction had gone on.

This is how it happens, you see: slowly, the celebratory cloth of gold starts unravelling, and the cheapness of the material of which it is contrived and woven becomes apparent. The heart is concealed under the clothes, and the survivalism under the eye-deceiving cultural tradition. But time and scepticism expose them. And one day, you act on what becomes clear to you.

In case you're wondering, I studied sociology, and psychology, and anthropology, and did further study, and am currently on track for tenure, but still suffer from imposter syndrome, as if I am guilty of some kind of fraudulent misrepresentation, nervously waiting to be found out. People still don't think my scholarly subject is objective, or credible or valid as a pursuit or vocation or any kind of contribution to human knowledge. They think I just make things up, as if all my research papers are just dressed up ways of processing my personal trauma.

Marriage strategies are my special field of interest. It's easy in South Asia, with its emphasis on the family rather than the individual and its obsession with spectacle, to practice personal deception and create a facsimile of apparent marital happiness. Many of us get married for the appearances of things, and what can be measured in scales and metric units and monetary calculations. To please our relatives, our intermediaries, and our ancestors. To augment our property portfolios. Our early romantic entanglements are neatly cut and spliced, and bundled away or hidden from sight, and we embark on a big charade, an open secret, like accomplices.

But of course the underlying crude, violent, primal hunger for prestige can never be satisfied in us. No brand names or designer labels, or cheap Instagrammable knockoffs can fill the anguish. Oh—it's a fire inside us, the desire to win, to pile up the accolades and trophies, to festoon our résumés, to name-drop the schools we go to, the colleges we attend, the private villas we holiday in: to glisten and glow, and parade our acquired prosperity in the all-judging, all-assessing, shrewdly scrutinising public eye.

And that unfortunate married man suffered from episodes of depression, and his cold-hearted marital partner left him alone every day, and every night. Too busy with her business meetings and meetups with the girls, and trips for social service organisations, and all the virtue signalling, to spend time at home.

Was she, I asked, clichéd as she was in every other way, unfaithful to the core promises she had publicly made on the day of the marriage, to care for him? (Seven times around the fire, and what a test that is.) Bowed down on her wedding day by sovereign gold jewellery that had come down to her through the women in her family, an easy and portable way to store up wealth, was she capable of something so banal as actual infidelity? So much energy is required by the pretence, that no residue is left for anything real.

My friend had accompanied his friend, her husband, on a shopping trip for his wife's birthday to the dazzling new hyper mall, where she had directed him to buy a yoga mat for her. The one he brought home was a trophy of vulgarity and cultural appropriation: when unrolled on the parquet floor, the mat, no doubt factory processed in some third-world sweatshop, was seen to be imprinted with the image of a white Western girl, levitating above a bed of lurid pink lotuses, in the Tree posture, improbably wearing a halter top with a slave choker.

That woman loved it, my friend said, rolling his eyes. The men on their shopping mission had been deceived by the lotuses on the edge of it, which was the only part of it that was visible when it was rolled up for sale in the store, along with its mass-marketed lookalikes.

Imagine how eroding and undermining it must have been: living with a person who showed you—every day—how little she desired your presence, and your company. It would have been hammered home to her husband every day of his life that he was not wanted, not wanted, not wanted: not valued for his conversation, for his company, for his ideas or any inconsequential, non-material contribution he could make—other than the stipend that manifested miraculously, mechanically—like clockwork—by electronic transfer, to enrich his wife's 'household money' allowance at the end of each month, when the interest from his parents' fixed term deposit funds came in.

She was continually ungrateful for absolutely everything that was given her: the refrigerator was too small, the SUV given to her was a 'shoddy' brand from South Korea, not the European one that she wanted, the apartment they were living in could have been better located in a more prestigious suburb where she could invite people she wanted to impress, et cetera, et cetera. Every picture tells a story, as the teachers used to tell us at school.

What a mockery of true marriage, I said to my cousin. It made me sad, and angry. He shrugged, and said, you get what you pay for. It was, after all, essentially a transaction. And she got what was—in her own eyes, blinded as they were by the lust for money—a bad bargain, and gave as bad as she got. She never saw the true value in him, his goodness of heart. And—after a while—he started to shrivel in plain sight. Because human beings are such vulnerable, responsive creatures, and sensitive to their environment and context. You can study sociology for years in prestigious universities and still never come close to solving a problem like this.

When Kamala Harris became the Vice President elect of the United States, this woman, that wife, with political ambitions herself, became vociferous on social media, claiming ancestral connections to her. I've seen her on Facebook, publicly speculating that her own mother was probably a distant cousin of this lady, but had not disclosed it before because divorce was a shameful thing in their family.

Kamala's mother had divorced her African husband in the US while Kamala and her sister were young children. She had then found sisterhood, support and shelter from the African American community, and identified personally with the civil rights movement as part of her own hybrid cultural identity. Her learned adaptability fused with her innate survival skills, and were invoked in her daughter's strategic, inclusive transcendence of rigid race and ethnic barriers, in the bid for relatability prior to the election.

The laughably flimsy claims of wannabe junior matriarchs tracing links with Kamala were an abrupt, short-lived, ephemeral social media phenomenon in South Asia, as actual facts about Kamala gradually became established, and displaced the wishful thinking and imaginative projections of those involved. Charlatans and opportunists come in all colours.

I could easily see that the virtue signalling woman who left her husband at home had a mania for performative piety, conducting her displays in the public gaze. Photos of her giving numerous donations of a thousand masks to under-resourced hospitals and myriad food packets to the picturesque poor adorned and embossed her social media. She founded a #MeToo-inspired Facebook group called 'Sisters Are Doing It For Themselves', just as fempowerment became fashionable.

In India, it was entertaining and deeply satisfying to see the celebrations of Diwali this year, where tributes to Kamala were made in effigy and painted in coloured powder in her mother's actual ancestral village, in an area which used to be known as Madras. She became a living goddess, symbol of universal Motherhood—in a place which her own mother had, ironically, clearly been determined to leave, to gain access to a better life.

Slowly, the silhouettes and cut-outs of our aspirations become substantiated through our repeated actions, over time. Like those transfers we used to use to illustrate our school projects when we were young. Position it, press hard and scribble on the back of the cut-out, and it appears in the space where you want it to be, like magic.

This is someone else's story. But in the deep weave of it, the truth resides.

Oh, I prayed during all the days of this recent Diwali—as I made our favourite sweets, and refreshed the flowers on the family altars, and lit the candles, and made sure we all wore the auspicious colours for each successive day—please Goddess, in your fiercest form, please burn down everything false: expose and destroy all man-made things which are indelibly stained, tainted and poisoned with human deceit, and human half-heartedness and hard-heartedness.

May that woman, and all those like her in character, suffer the torment of never getting what she wants: may the wealth she strives for—and exploits people for—elude her. May the virtues of the people she tries to take advantage of, confound her and rebound on her. May retribution come, in its full karmic glory, and engulf and overthrow her. May all the impurities be burned out of her character. And if you do this, be assured that I, too, will be in line to light that flame.

May all false histories die, may all untrue stories—and those who tell them—wither and perish. Break them down, Mother! Destroy them and topple those atrophied, exhausted, white-anted facades that have been established on base injustice, cruelty, avarice and fraudulence. Let's get to the real roots of the matter, with every sharpened instrument to which we have access.

Kiewa Creek Diary

Sharon Rundle

Sunday, 1 February

The day dawns. Sulphur-crested cockatoos shriek as they rise from the trees. Startled kookaburras call out in raucous laughter and baby magpies squawk.

By mid-morning, heat and humidity drive the locals to the spring-fed creek that bubbles and babbles through the village. Cicadas are in full chorus. Kiewa Creek is awash with adults, school children, toddlers and babies. Depending on which part of the meandering creek they choose, the locals are diving, swimming, floating on inflatable plastic pool toys. A few family dogs join in. The air fills with the sound of squeals, laughter and excited barking, as the locals frolic in cool, pristine water.

The Riparian Regeneration Group, a volunteer committee dedicated to cleaning, weeding and regenerating the banks along the creek, is also ready for a quick dip by mid-afternoon. At the local general store—called the Trading Post because it is also a co-operative for local producers—the manager orders supplies of sunscreen, sunglasses, personal insect repellent and sunburn relief. He stocks locally made hats woven from reeds, hemp fibre and softened cane.

Kiewa Creek is the spot to be, and many stay well into star-studded summer evenings to swim, or relax on towels covering patchy kangaroo grass, before reluctantly heading for home. Even the odd hermit in the hills comes down to cool off in the creek at night. Koalas dogpaddle across to find choicer gum leaves or a new mate, and wombats and wallabies drink and dart about. After dark, the creek is an orchestra pit of frogs croaking, crickets rubbing, nightjars calling 'whook, whook' and the low haunting hoots of tawny frogmouths.

Kiewa means 'clear water' in the local Indigenous language and the creek is the lifeline of the village, landscape and wildlife.

Sunday, 8 February

Night owls living on higher slopes above the creek watch a vapour exude from the trees and plants. It gathers into a cloud and slowly sinks until it hovers just above the creek.

Dawn breaks above the cloud in the gully. As if drawn by sunbeams, thick mist rises from the cloud floating over the creek and drifts higher and higher until the trails of white clouds dissolve.

Heat and humidity encourage the locals to immerse themselves in the flowing creek, cooled by crystal-clear springs gurgling up from a water table deep below. Children are collecting cicada shells.

'Look, there's a yellow Monday here coming out of its shell', a small boy calls out.

'I spotted a greengrocer, a floury baker *and* a black prince.'

Another child creeps up to her mother and surreptitiously sticks cicada shells to her T-shirt, then shrieks with laughter and gives the game away.

'What do we do when we see a brown snake?' one of the Riparian Regeneration Group volunteers asks the children.

'Keep still and don't bother the snake', they chorus.

The RRG is a loosely organised mix of mums and dads, retirees, even a few 'weekenders' who drive up from the city. They have no hierarchy, no affiliation, incorporation, registration or insurance, but nevertheless they clean up litter, remove weeds, whipper-snip the grasses and keep the place in good order. Some have qualifications and know how to plant sympathetic flora and grasses to prevent erosion and give stability to the soil on the creek banks and steeper slopes of the gully. They study the best preservation methods for the shady tree canopy, made up of river gums, eucalypts, acacias, casuarinas and angophoras. They keep the landscape well-watered in times of drought.

On summer afternoons, when school ends, the widest shallowest stretch of creek becomes the next playground as the younger children run or cycle down to the water. Homemade boats created from paddle-pop sticks with paper sails skim along. Toddlers paddle and scoop water, sand and smooth stones washed up from the creek bed into plastic buckets and bowls. When the high school bus arrives from the nearest town, the older kids stream off wearing swimmers under their uniforms. They head for deeper water and whoop loudly as it hits their skin. They shout and splash about until parents heading homeward call to them.

The Riparian Regeneration Group keeps an informal eye on proceedings over the course of the day, sometimes acting as referees, as they rake leaves to add to the compost covering the roots of trees or remove gold-maned dandelions and rosettes of heart-shaped oxalis leaves, seeded and fertilised by birds. Everyone keeps alert for any sign of smoke.

Even the village book club becomes a floating fiction group as the mercury continues to soar. Swimwear is the most practical choice for a relaxed discussion. The mosquitoes are not out in the plague proportions of the early summer and warm nights keep locals at the creek for longer than usual. Some families picnic on the creek banks instead of cooking meals in steamy kitchens.

Under a full moon, the silvery creek takes on a life of its own.

Sunday, 15 February

When the first few toddlers become ill, the common symptoms are irritation of the eye, skin and throat. Various tests come back negative but by the time the results arrive, pre-schoolers have succumbed to these same symptoms. Dr Andrew, the village GP, gives a primary diagnosis and prescriptions for local cortisone applications or antihistamines. Parents, needless to say, are worried about this mysterious illness. The Trading Post sells its entire stock of cough and cold syrup, antihistamines, eye drops, vapour rub, calamine lotion, Condy's crystals and other home remedies.

A few days later, some of the older residents come down with similar symptoms. The heat and humidity show no sign of abating and only make the locals feel worse. Soaking in the cool creek water brings temporary relief, at least. Locals compare symptoms. Some of the Riparian Regeneration volunteers wonder if the problems could be caused by an allergic reaction to one of the plants, grasses or weeds growing on the banks of the creek. All the group's work is done by hand. No one uses pesticide or chemicals.

Dr Andrew is at a loss. The skin rashes and associated cough and watery eyes usually indicate measles or some other infectious process. This urticarial type of rash, raised and streaky like hives, which worsens if scratched, suggests allergies of some sort. But so far no one has enlarged glands. Then again, it could be a form of dermatitis—but with increasing presentations, alarm bells are ringing. He reads through medical books, checks online and confers with colleagues but the eye problems, skin rashes and respiratory irritation continue to mystify him. Harry, the manager of the Trading Post, orders additional supplies. Parents are anxious. Nobody knows how the illness is spread.

In the late afternoon, shafts of golden sunlight penetrate the canopy to illuminate the creek below and create rainbows from the spray. Discussion continues as the locals gather around their favourite waterhole. At sunset, a sentinel cocky calls out to the stragglers in his flock as they fly back for the night. Cicada song comes to an abrupt halt. The sky turns pink, orange and purple as the sun melts on the horizon.

After dark, a cool breeze shakes the canopy and moonlight filters through the branches, creating patterns in the silhouette.

Sunday, 22 February

The wait continues for Ministry of Health results and analyses, and some of the senior residents develop secondary illnesses. Every member of the Riparian Regeneration Group is affected. The Trading Post orders fresh batches of over-the-counter medications in bulk. Some family dogs scratch so furiously they rip out their hair. The local vet takes her own samples and prescribes cortisone ointment in the meantime. Rumours fly thick and fast.

A few children develop lesions which become infected from constant scratching. Harry orders boxes of manicure scissors and cotton gloves, though keeping these on the hands of small children in a heatwave is not easy. The local primary school closes temporarily. Parents' schedules are thrown into chaos.

Much to the students' disgust, classes continue as normal at the high school, since there has been no confirmation that the illness is anything out of the ordinary. Nobody wants to spread alarm by mentioning isolation. Teachers keep a supply of soothing lotions and throat lozenges for their classes and themselves, and wash their hands religiously.

Dr Andrew advises his patients to send off samples of spring water, bore water and even rainwater from tanks to the Department of Agriculture. Selena, the primary school principal, does the same for the school water sources. For the first time in memory, Harry at the Trading Post adds bottled water and antibacterial hand cleaning gel and wipes to his next order.

On a restless, moonless night, the mostly peaceful village becomes a hotbed of gossip, accusations and conspiracy theories, as locals debate the source of this unwelcome outbreak.

Sunday, 1 March

The air is suffocating. Weather forecasts indicate a ridge of high pressure hovering over the area. What with the discomfort of their symptoms, the heat, and pitching in with child-minding, Riparian Regeneration Group volunteers are thin on the ground. Leaves pile up on the tracks and creek banks. The remaining volunteers resort to using leaf blowers, which scare the birds. They pump water from the creek to hose the leaf litter covering tree roots to protect them from the searing midday sun. Perspiration flows in tiny tributaries as the few willing workers try to tend to the landscape.

Some children recover while others become worse. No word yet from the Ministry of Health about the source or cause of the outbreak.

Selena, the primary school principal, notices that dragonflies no longer skim the creek. She collects and sends off samples of creek water, riparian plants and soil to colleagues at the CSIRO. Born and raised at Kiewa Creek, Selena trained in ecology and founded the Riparian Regeneration Group. Her enthusiasm sparked the village's interest in studying and caring for the creek and its surrounds. She continues to be a motivating force in the community.

Under a high dome of cloudless sky, Kiewa Creek is a shady oasis of relief from draining heat and burning irritation. Lying in the shallows to read or gossip or watch over small children is still a favourite pastime.

Sunday, 8 March

Government officials appear in the village, poking in their noses and asking questions. Apparently some of them are doctors. Gossip ratchets up a few notches. The words 'disease' and 'infection'—even 'Ebola'—circulate. Residents scratch their heads as they struggle to remember anybody who has been on holiday or had visitors lately and speculate about 'weekenders' who may have visited foreign shores. Selena and Dr Andrew stave off questions.

'Are you going to tell us what's going on?'

'Why are we being treated like idiots?'

'Will our kids be okay?'

'Not to mention the rest of us, we're all worried here.'

'We can't say yet', says Dr Andrew. 'The wrong information won't do you any good. Please be patient.'

The officials won't reveal their reasons for visiting this small community that's so unremarkable it's difficult even to find on a map. Except for approvals of development applications to build homes, the regular rate notices and maintenance on the main roads before state government elections, the place is normally all but forgotten by all three tiers of government.

The Riparian Regeneration Group is invited to participate in 'voluntary interviews', in which they are grilled by officials. Even after answering the questions, the volunteers are no wiser as to the reason for the investigation, though some say they recall an unusual odour of aniseed or liquorice at the creek lately. Swabs are taken from the cabins and trays of utes and trucks in the local area. Car boots are searched. The officials interview the manager of the Trading Post.

'We need a list of anyone who has bought liquid fertiliser, chemicals, or containers for such products.'

'It'll take a couple of days to go through the receipts, but I can get the information you need', Harry says. 'What's the time frame?'

'We'll start with the past month and work back from there.'

Harry nods.

'And do us a favour, don't go telling everyone about this.'

On the surface, life is going on as usual—but suspicion, slander and superstition are rife. Locals brood over the continuing outbreaks of skin and throat irritations, and the peculiar interest of the government in their neck of the woods.

Sunday, 15 March

A cool change blows through the village. It feels like autumn. The window of the Trading Post displays firelighters, tins of powdered chocolate and packets of marshmallows, as well as locally designed and knitted beanies and scarves.

Selena leaves for the city, to confer with her colleagues and get to the bottom of this sudden government interest in her community.

Dr Andrew contacts the Ministry of Health. The reports he should have had days ago still haven't arrived.

Fewer volunteers and a drop in air temperature mean less activity down at the creek, though the weather is mild enough for a dip during the middle of the day. Naturally, the children still flock to the water—one of their favourite haunts.

Sunday, 22 March

In the dark of the moon, two babies and three toddlers are sent to the children's hospital in the city. Their infections have become serious.

Selena visits Dr Andrew on her return from the city. They ask all residents and visitors to attend a public meeting at the school next Sunday morning.

Locals also receive letters from the Ministry of Health advising of an information session next Sunday, which they will hold at the public school hall. In the meantime, the creek is under a safety assessment and off-limits to all except authorised personnel.

Riparian Regeneration Group volunteers wear protective clothing as they erect barriers and signs with a skull and crossbones symbol along the creek banks.

Apart from avoiding the creek, residents continue to live as normally as they can. Gossip goes on unabated. Everyone has a theory, a solution or a cure, if only people would listen.

Discussions continue long into the night outside the Trading Post and Harry obliges by closing the shop later and later.

Dr Andrew warns against using alternative therapies until it is clear what they are dealing with. People are more circumspect after that. Harry optimistically orders Easter eggs in shiny foil, along with extra groceries for the holiday period, then adds more home remedies and comfort items to the list.

Sunday, 29 March

The number of visiting officials and their staff grows. Police officers arrive to investigate the problem. Everyone but the hermits is interviewed. Medics from the Ministry take over Dr Andrew's rooms. Specialists prod and pinch and paint the 112 local residents with potions. Assessors from the Department of Agriculture check local produce and water supplies. Journalists arrive to investigate the cause of all the activity.

Caravans are parked alongside the creek. The visitors commandeer a mobile canteen and set it up on the oval.

In a show of solidarity with the residents, Harry at the Trading Post increases his standing order for supplies of fresh fruit and vegetables, eggs, and prettily decorated jars of honey and preserves from local producers, and readjusts his order for alcohol.

Everyone in the village attends the public meeting called by Dr Andrew and Selena. Even the hermits appear and hover in the doorway. The principal's expression is sombre as she announces the results of her independent inquiry and her analysis of samples taken in and around the creek, subject to official confirmation by the experts.

'Not long after the New Year, a spill occurred upstream in Kiewa Creek', Selena says to the worried locals. 'It went unnoticed and unreported. While the source of the spill and the exact composition is still under investigation, it appears to have affected our community. My own investigation implicates a chemical compound often used for coal cleaning. Whether it leaked accidentally or was dumped waste, is still to be confirmed.'

She looks to Dr Andrew.

'So far, bore water and tank water tested is clear', he says. 'But you should wash all produce thoroughly with bottled water and use bottled water for drinking and cleaning teeth for the time being. At least until official clearance is given.

'As a precaution, the creek, creek banks and several hundred metres either side are declared strictly out of bounds until further notice. The pristine springs should help dilute the spill, if it hasn't seeped through to the water table.'

A ripple runs through the hall. Dr Andrew continues.

'It looks as if the health problems will be temporary for most. All the symptoms suffered fit Selena's hypothesis. While there is no specific data on the toxic effects of this chemical compound—no known long-term carcinogenic effects or developmental toxicity—it is noted that it may cause harm if ingested or inhaled. It may have adverse effects for those with suppressed immune systems. But those who have been hospitalised are improving and are expected to recover.'

The afternoon meeting called by the Ministry of Health is less straightforward. The locals sense a cover-up as officious public servants beat around the bush and fend off questions, while insisting that all is under control, that the creek will be properly fenced and sealed off, and that a crisis management team will assist residents. When the question is raised of compulsory or forced evacuation, the information providers clam up. One moron jokes that the reports state that their exposure to small amounts of a chemical diluted in creek water will not cause residents to drop dead any time soon. A senior medic frowns and advises everyone to avoid the creek and to drink and use only bottled water because at this point in time it is the sensible thing to do.

Complimentary bottles of water are handed out. Selena wants to know who will collect and dispose of the mountain of empty plastic bottles piling up in the school recycling skip. She tells the officials that everyone in this community is responsible for disposal of their own rubbish and waste, there is no council collection service.

Sunday, 5 April

Easter Sunday. The sun is shining, and a few residents drive off to a church or club in town or to the Easter holiday markets. At home, parents hide Easter eggs for excited children. Nobody has friends or relatives visiting this year. Even the weekenders are keeping away.

All week, Kiewa Creek teemed with anonymous figures in hazmat outfits, some putting up permanent barriers and signage, others taking more samples from the creek and surrounds.

In a few days, results will confirm the spill, its extent, how far it has leached into the creek bed and whether it has affected the effervescent springs from the water table deep below. The official results from testing bore and tank water will be available. Arborists are coming to check the state of the trees and plants, once the level of contamination is established.

The locals try their best to stay calm and carry on but the jitters don't subside easily. No spume, no discolouration, no obvious sign of adulteration can be seen with the naked eye. Kiewa Creek is eerily silent and the water remains crystal clear as it snakes its way through the valley.

Dissembling Fraud

Direct Action

Cate Kennedy

Direct action. You don't want to hear it. You want to make another pot of tea, and wait for *Star Trek: The Next Generation* to come on. Direct action means arguing with punters on the street who try to pull your placards off you, and dancing round the missile base so that the cops can laugh themselves sick before they move in on you. It's something you admire hearing about second-hand, shaking your head at someone else's bruises. It's not something you feel like doing, on a cold winter's night after dinner. Except that you can't stop thinking that right now, after dinner or not, and all through tonight, and tomorrow, twenty-four hours a day, in fact, seven days a week, Barron Paper Mills, just up the road, are glugging industrial effluent straight into the river.

Picketing? The laundry is full of pickets. STOP TOXIC SPILL, they say. THE PLANET IS NOT YOUR TOILET. And so on. Barron executives, accustomed to paying big dollars to give toilet paper a good image, have an Environmental Impact Study saying that the effluent falls within acceptable levels of toxic contamination. Life seems full of acceptable levels now. I myself fall into the acceptable level of thirteen per cent of qualified tradespeople unable to find employment.

I've stood knee-deep in the sludge twenty metres down from the dual-emission outlet pipes and been asked by well-pressed retirees just off to the pokies why I haven't got a job. *Because they've closed. They laid me off. I worked for four years, let me show you my certificate and union card.* No point screaming. No point even answering. There's a photo of us 'Direct Action' campaigners, cut out of the local rag and brown and oil-splattered now, on the fridge. We look puny and pale in our rolled-up jeans, holding dead fish, and every time I pass it I can't help cringing at the headline 'Ecowarriors'—saving the public the trouble of jeering at us by doing it myself.

I observe the comforting sight of the Enterprise going where no one has gone before (used to be no *man* but see how non-sexism has changed the world), sip my tea and watch Riker dispensing Klingons. Glug, glug, goes the effluent two kilometres away, unstoppable, poisonous, irreversible. This time of night it slows to a trickle, by 9.30 in the morning it's like the North Sea pipeline.

'I'm providing jobs', the executive from Barron had argued with me as I stood in the river that morning, knowing where to hit the nerve. I had an answer ready but couldn't trust my voice, or my hand holding the rotting fish. He'd sneered at my 'Vegetarians of the World Unite' T-shirt.

'Sure you've got your priorities straight, son?' he'd said, and when I still didn't answer, he'd said, 'Come on, speak up, moron', and I'd thrown the fish, and there'd been trouble.

Sometimes Monday mornings I still jump awake at 6.45 and go to roll out of bed before realising there's no whistle to get up for. It'd be a long bike ride to work anyway, even if I'd kept my job, since the factory is now in Macau. Some other poor bastard's starting up the oxytorch now, checking his mask and checking his back. People used to ask for me at the workshop. 'Get a skill and you'll always be in demand', is something my dad used to say, and he believed it too, until they retired him. He says he doesn't miss the work. Tells me this in the middle of his shed, which has more tools in it than Mitre 10. His face lighting up when a neighbour brings their car over, hurrying for a spanner, telling them it's no trouble.

'Cheer up, Gaz', is what he says now. 'It's not you, son. There'll be an opening for a skilled bloke sooner or later.'

I have a plan. My only visible direct action thus far is stepping for the first time in fourteen years into a butcher shop. Two dollars' worth of bones, paper bag please, not plastic. I go every day for two weeks. The butcher becomes my friend. All day he bashes up the carcasses of dead things, and I've never seen the smile off his face. Now there's a puzzle for you.

'Dad', I say, 'I need to borrow the oxy.'

His face brightens. He heaves himself off the Recliner Rocker. 'Got a job on, son?'

'Kind of.'

'That's the way.' He pads out to the shed, checks the set in the box.

'You wouldn't have a few bits of steel plate lying around, would you?'

'How big?'

I indicate with my hands.

He stops, thinks. 'I just might, out the back.'

My dad, recycler since 1963. He returns, his arms weighted.

'You could patch a hole on the *Queen Mary* with these.'

'Just about.'

'Hang about while I get you a couple of welding rods.'

He putters about, putting his hand on everything he wants, competent, cheerful. He would have had fifteen years more productive time in him at the garage, given a chance. He could have trained the apprentice who replaced him. Now he is on the scrapheap, and his response is to make something useful with the scrap.

'I think the bottle's pretty full', he says, checking it.

'Great. Thanks.'

'Good on yer, Gary. It's like I told you—there's always an opening for a bloke with skills.'

'One or two, still', I say, hefting the box.

And I'm almost at the door before he says in a voice just a degree or two cooler, 'So, what's the job, then?'

Sprung, I turn around and walk back.

'Remember that time we went fishing in the Hootie?'

'Sure I do.' He's fiddling with the welding rod, putting it into the vice, turning the handle. Listening.

'Remember when I caught that brown trout?'

There are things I hope my father remembers from my childhood; about three big things. One was the day he pushed me off, minus training wheels, on my first two-wheeler—a low-slung green dragster—and suddenly I was steering and pedalling and the bike was staying upright, and I sneaked a quick look behind me and my dad was jumping down the track, punching the air with triumph. Another time was when I'd fixed a tiny leak in our Clarke's backyard swimming pool with my bike repair kit. My father had taken a few short steps towards the repair, stopped, considered, and looked at me with what an eight-year-old boy could only take for respect.

And, last of all, in lit-up focus in my memory, there was the fishing. Me with my rod from Santa, my father with an old rubber lure designed to catch a fourteen-pound Murray cod on the South Australian rivers in the 1950s. Did I tell you he never threw anything away?

We had been fishing for an hour, not saying anything, when there was a bang on my rod like a bailiff's knock and the K-mart plastic bent like a horseshoe and my father whooped with sudden childlike excitement. His hands flew out to grab the rod, then slowly went back into his pockets, where they rolled and twitched as he instructed me how to reel the fish in, his teeth clenched. It was a big brown trout, just about the most beautiful thing I'd ever seen, and my father's 'you little *beauty*' fell on my head like a benediction.

The trout lay there drowning in the air, and I could see the miraculous gills opening and closing, its eyes moving as it gulped the wrong element, two old scars on its big mottled back, and then everything slowed down and I reached my fingers, fumbling with agonised realisation, into the trout's mouth to get that hook out, and I snatched the fish up in both hands and threw it back into the water. The absolutely silent moments when it was flexing and shining in the air over the brown water lasted for years, and while I waited for it to hit I felt something come loose in my chest, emerge, test the air and flap away in big white beats.

I want my father to remember this day, the last day I ever fished.

'There aren't any brown trout in the Hootie now, dad.'

He examines the edge on a chisel, rubs it up and down a scar on his thumb. 'There's not much of anything anymore, son. Not that kind of thing.'

'They're pouring emission straight into the water down there, from two pipes hanging out over the bank.'

He tests the chisel, nodding slowly as he works out what I want his welding gear for. 'They're pouring human shit straight into the ocean, too', he says, pinning me with a glance, 'but I haven't noticed you welding your arse shut.'

The moment twists in the air, seconds away from the wet smack of too late.

'If you're not going to lend it to me, just say.'

He slides the chisel carefully back into its slot in his box. Sighs. Fumbles for the metre to check the levels in the acetylene tank.

Rome was attacked by Gallic troops in 390 BC and what raised the alarm that saved the city? Geese. The holy geese in the city's temple started up and the invaders couldn't quieten them and Rome woke up to itself. I read this in an article titled 'Microlivestock: Little-known Small Animals with a Promising Economic Future', along with the information that geese are used now to guard missile bases in Europe. Geese. They just raise the alarm and gabble away and don't shut up, and you would be mistaken if you didn't take that seriously, standing there with your sabotage tools and camouflage gear on. This is the kind of information I would never have learned about in my old job. You get a fair bit of reading in when you're unemployed.

Barron's four German Shepherds bounce down to the fence when they see me, the bringer of midnight snacks for two weeks. Barron Paper Mills has made two great mistakes in the protection of its plant. One, it has installed dogs of a famously aggressive breed, but it has neglected to train them because it thinks their presence is a deterrent in itself. Two, they have fed these dogs on dry dog-kibble and water. The first night I pushed four kilos of lamb shanks through the wire, the dogs' barking switched off like someone had pulled the plug. They glanced up at me as they dropped their heads to it with a look so sentient, so conspiratorial, it was breathtaking. One of them, I swear, winked.

Fourteen nights later, our transaction is as businesslike as a drug deal. Through the cyclone-wire mesh goes eight kilos of beef ribs sliced up on the butcher's bandsaw. Inside the nightwatchman's room, the guard sleeps through *Letterman*. The bark of the dogs would wake him. But the dogs don't bark. They're dumb, but not that dumb. They give me quick leery dog smiles. I am Dog Santa. Then they barrel off into the darkness, meat and drool trailing from their mouths. I cut the wire close to a pole, where the flap snaps back invisibly. Barron, you should have invested in geese.

As I move just inside the lights on the fence perimeters, behind the factory towards the pipeline, I'm thinking of my father's hands, pushed down into his pockets like he was holding down foam buoys, clenching and jumping in there, torn between taking something and giving it away. The fingers that could reach in behind a spinning fanbelt and locate a nut and adjust it precisely. My own hands that used to be hard with a smattering of burns and marks but now are soft, with clean fingernails. Want to know what someone does for a living, check their hands. Hold out yours, shake theirs, and you'll know everything you need to know. I'm puffing, out of condition, fingers tired already from just cutting the wire. Watch out world, here comes Mr Activist.

Hoisting myself down through blackberries to the pipes, I breathe easier now, 150 metres from the building. The oxy, when I light it, sounds a solid hiss of hot energy, like a gas lamp out in the bush—loud as a roar, it seems to me. I turn the flame, pull down my mask. It smells like an honest day's work, a smell I haven't quite forgotten yet.

It takes me an hour, but I was never one to rush a job. I lean into the blackberries, my boot wedged into poisoned riverbank. Those radiant blue chips waterfall off the metal like the fireworks we used to nail to the fence back before you needed to be a qualified pyrotechnician to handle them. Catherine wheels, spinning molten stars, my mum lighting the whole packet, every one different.

My back starts to protest and the scratches down my legs smoulder. I know what I'm doing, though. I'm welding metal together, watching the solder grey and cool in a neat permanent join even as I move to the next section, twisted around a waste pipe in the darkness, hearing the liquid inside sizzle against the heat as the pipe fills slowly, finishing off the second plate, hunched against a riverbank I once caught a fish off. By tomorrow morning, the guy I threw the fish at will crank up his machinery and things will slowly seize in a white-hot and expensive flooding. His ruined two-hundred-dollar shoes will splash him out of the swill, into head office to call the police.

Stepping back now around the manicured grass, every second expecting the sliding blue and red lights of a cop car and the android crackle of their voices over the radios to greet me at the road, I swallow nothing again and again. The taste of nickel, of smoking solder in my mouth. But there is just the night there, grey and woolly and incomprehensible like I've just woken up into it. I'm still wearing my welding mask, hobbling as the muscles in my legs start stiffening up. The dogs, breathing meaty breath onto me, fawn around, coming out of the darkness and leaping up at me, their brains addled with protein and low-IQ self-interest. I am covered with oily sludge from the emission pipes, and saliva from the sated dogs.

Barron, neglecting dog training, did however splash out on surveillance cameras. As I unwittingly pass one's red-eyed field of vision I am thinking only of getting home. But two days later in the paper there is a blurry photo of something that looks like Bigfoot under a story in which Barron executives cite figures that they say have cost the whole community dearly. Mindless and malicious sabotage that affects the reputation of Australian business both at home and abroad. They cite their Environmental Impact Study, their acceptable levels, their state-of-the-art corporate workplace agreement policies.

The cops take one look at the job, and start looking for welders with a history of disturbing the peace.

It's a small field of contenders, and it doesn't take them long.

They have the photo when they come over to my place, and one of them looks at it and gives a little smile at the blurry figure emerging out of the dark in the big, black welding mask, both hands raised and holding cylinders. I know what he is thinking. The resemblance has struck me, too.

'Stand and deliver, eh?' he says to me, and we both grin. He's the kind of bloke I'd buy a beer.

'Tell 'em I died game', I say. I get a ride in a police car for my trouble.

Outside the court, what the press is fond of calling a small but vocal group of protestors has assembled, and the posters out of the laundry are in action again. There is ragged cheering as I make my way through.

There have been questions, which Barron's media releases have answered with an increasing note of self-righteousness. The press aren't given a gift like this—a toilet-paper manufacturer—every day, and they don't waste it. There are also headlines in the 'Something Fishy?' vein, showing journalists frowning thoughtfully at a high-tide mark of solid scum. Barron execs have posed nervously for photos around the new pipes with filter attachments and released their sudden altruistic intention to create a waterbird sanctuary upstream, but their spin doctors, deep into damage control, have kicked a bit of an own goal with their new slogan.

'We're here to clean up!' doesn't do them any favours at all.

Me, I am dubbed 'The Man of Steel'. I am in the Odd Spot.

'Name?' I am asked in the courtroom.

'Gary Sutherland.'

'And your profession?'

'Welder.'

The prosecutor gives me a *now-come-on* look. 'Wouldn't it be more correct to say you are unemployed?'

'Yes, I am unemployed.'

'And have been on unemployment benefits for well over two years?'

It's funny, but I'm not even angry. 'It would be more correct to say I am a qualified welder', I say, 'who does not have a job.'

As they read the charge, the noise outside increases into one of those clapping call-and-response chants. From inside it sounds a bit like a herd of distant honking, just between you and me. I smile.

The river doesn't look any cleaner. Some days green algae makes it look solid as a billiard table; some days it's black as Ned Kelly's eyes. There will still never be any fish in it. That part of our lives is over, mostly. This is what occurs to me as I am charged that day in court: that there aren't enough moments of fumbling to pull out the hook, our hands no longer move independently of our heads. But as I walk out, I catch sight of my father, down the back, head up, worth ten of the bastards in suits. The look he has in his eye is not the one he had when I caught the fish.

It is the look he had when I let the fish go.

Shadow Box

Anne Benjamin

Uma stopped. Right there, in the middle of the crossing outside the station. A grey-suited man strode headlong into her back.

'Watch it', he growled. Uma was waving both arms in the air, her big soft brown bag flying around. The man turned back to stare at the stocky dark woman, with grey curls and wearing purple baggy pants and red floral puffer jacket, who seemed to be talking to a billboard that rose above the opposite pavement. *Vote* SALLY ELING. *A representative you can trust.* He shook his head and continued on.

'The resurrection of the whitened sepulchre', Uma crowed. She gave the billboard the finger and huffed her way across the intersection.

Today was her sixtieth birthday. The staff at the refuge were putting on a lunch. The billboard rattled her memories, but nothing was going to spoil today.

Uma had arrived in Sydney a few months after her wedding to Ajit, bringing a brand-new postgraduate degree in social work and enough stainless-steel vessels to clutter the tiny kitchen in their Ashfield flat. Ajit continued his work as an engineer in a construction company, while Uma settled into life as a housewife. Having left her home state of Kerala to study at Stella Maris in Chennai, she was used to making new friends in the diverse neighbourhood in which she'd landed. She was blunt and talkative, free with her opinions and occasionally Ajit needed to smooth over relations with friends who'd been offended by Uma's insistence on her own opinion. When, a year later, to the satisfaction of family elders and their own delight, a son was born, Ajit hoped Uma's absorption with the baby would lead to a moderation in the offences she caused.

Janak blossomed, alert and intelligent, under Uma's attention and Ajit's pride. It was around ten in the morning, full of sunshine and wind, one day in late August. She was hanging washing on the communal clothesline, snatching space for their clothes ahead of other residents. Plump three-year-old Janak was playing between wet sheets, annoying Uma, in case he grubbied them, and she was hurrying to get the job done. Ajit had left for work as usual around seven: there was a construction site with some problems; an assessment needed to be made. Somewhere in the city.

She heard the phone ringing as she unlocked the door. It rang off. She shrugged and made herself a cup of coffee, boiling the milk on the electric stove and letting it rise in a froth before she poured it back and forth from saucepan to cup. Janak was playing quietly on the floor. She sat and inhaled the steamy comfort of the coffee.

Someone knocked. At the door, two policemen—one young, big and awkward, the other older and grave—asked to come inside. She hesitated. For one magnified moment, she paused in the pleasure of sunshine, completed chores, a happy child, the nostalgic aroma of brewed coffee, holding off the one that was to follow. The face of the older man was telling her something: Ajit?

'You are Mrs Nayar? Mrs Ajit Nayar?' There'd been an accident. A wall had fallen. 'We regret, madam… your husband. Under the masonry. No one else, er, fortunately, er, dead, madam. Some injured. Do you have any family members you can call?' She waited till they left. Then her howl rang up the stairwell, echoing over and over.

She was a widow at twenty-seven with a child to raise. She would need to work. She didn't mind that. Being boxed up in a two-bedroom flat did not suit her. She freshened up her CV, confident that her qualifications were more than enough to find something worthwhile that would support her and Janak. She was not prepared for the responses to her carefully crafted applications.

'Your local work experience?' 'Local references?' 'A master's degree? Really? Perhaps you should look somewhere else.'

So she completed the public service exam and was offered a position as clerical assistant in the Department of Social Services.

She became a regular volunteer at a refuge for young women in the city, assisting with meals and occasional counselling. She balanced her caring for Janak, full-time work and her determination to expand her repertoire of skills against the need for friends. After two years, the company's compensation payment gave her enough to purchase an apartment at West Ryde, further from the city, but affordable. When Janak started school, she transferred to a higher grade with the Police Department. She completed a course in business administration and took a professional officer position in the Department of Justice. She rounded her study off with a diploma in public sector management.

By the time she was in her mid-fifties, Uma had been in the Department of Infrastructure and Development for nearly ten years. Janak had graduated and was practising law with a large firm of international consultants. By dint of diligence and her pedantic attention to details and protocols, she had earned a senior role in the finance division. Regarded by some as too eccentric to be popular, her professionalism was respected. Her juniors knew she would monitor accounts and reports zealously. They laughed at her mannerisms behind her back and worked to the standards she expected.

It was around this time that Sally Eling became head of the department. Sally was coiffured, trendy and elegant and brought an unconventional approach to management. She made it clear that she wasn't worried about timesheets and long lunch breaks, arguing that it was good for morale. 'All work and no play', she would laugh, tossing her shoulder-length dyed black hair and fluttering cherry-enamelled fingertips in the air. She modelled this with her own regular extended lunches. Sally had been in the role for about three months when the head of the finance division and Uma's immediate boss announced his retirement. In Uma's mind, Neville Smith was the ultimate public servant, combining all she admired by way of diligence, propriety and professionalism. He and Sally were poles apart, yet he reported to her with the respect he had offered all his superiors over forty years of service.

Uma asked him bluntly, 'Why are you going, Neville? It's too soon.'

His reply was the one he gave to everyone, 'It's the right time for me.' This did not satisfy Uma completely, but she knew Neville kept his own counsel. In the interim awaiting his replacement, Uma was appointed as acting head of finance.

Uma sat before the screen. She was perplexed. She wished Neville was around so she could ask his advice. She knew she could rely on that. She was seeing a pattern that she couldn't quite comprehend. A number of contracts issued in the previous year had been signed off and closed. The contracts—one for scoping a programme of maintenance for several state-owned properties, one for landscaping, one for development of a regeneration project—had been paid in full. She'd checked the accounts. In each case, the acquittal report merely said, 'Contract Suspended'. No further note. No explanation. She re-checked—$3,075,500 paid in total. Three million. And no proper acquittal or refunding. Someone had slipped up.

She asked her PA, Steph, to double-check the files and figures for her. Steph brought them back, cheerful as ever, 'You're absolutely right, boss. That's it, cancelled and closed.'

'Thanks, Steph', Uma mumbled, still staring at the pages sprawled across her desk. 'And I've said, don't call me "boss".' Steph grinned.

Sally was wearing a lime green linen sheath that showed off her figure the day Uma spoke to her about the contracts. The department head crossed her tapered legs.

'Let me see, I'll look into it. By the way', she added as Uma, in what had become her regular dress of slacks and loose bulky tops, stood to leave, 'Where do you buy your clothes, Uma? You know, you're still quite young.' She proceeded to suggest that Uma might present herself in a way that was, well, a little less drab. A little lipstick, maybe. As she was still speaking, Sally freshened up her own dark plum lip gloss. She stood up, grabbing her purse and jacket. 'Excuse me. My lunch date has arrived', she nodded towards the open area of the office.

Uma recognised Richard, 'Sally's squeeze', as Steph described him, in his corduroy slacks, white turtleneck and tweed jacket. He was handsome in that affluent kind of way that her father used to refer to back home as a 'ghee finish'. Uma stood back to let Sally leave.

A few weeks later, Uma was relieved when Neville's replacement arrived, and she could slide back into her normal role. The new head of finance, Andrew Younan, was young and energetic, friendly to staff.

'Did Sally mention the contracts?' she asked him after he'd been there a few weeks.

'What contracts?'

'Three contracts that were paid out and terminated without completion?'

Andrew looked blank. 'Nope', he said. 'I'll check with her.'

There was another thing she wanted to raise with Andrew, something that was disturbing her about the credit card expenses used by Sally. Uma had learned from Neville to attend to details. It suited her tendency to scrupulosity. There were expenses there that had never appeared previously, and Uma wondered if somehow, in replacing the outgoing male head of department, Sally had negotiated to include things like entertaining, dry-cleaning, beauty treatments, and well-being massages.

I suppose there is an argument, she mused, for her being able to carry her responsibilities better if she is feeling relaxed, but... She continued to monitor the credit card expenses closely.

A month passed. One Friday morning, as Uma waited on the platform for the 7.15 train to the city, she was hit by dizziness. A sense of falling. The steel rails vibrated as the train approached. She dreaded the working day ahead. Her sense that she had failed to deal with the credit card issue poured petrol on her guilt. And she was angry that other people's actions put her in this situation. Her depressive predisposition was a fissure in her compulsion to do everything perfectly. It had morphed into a constant shadow since the day Ajit had died: the day she'd argued bitterly with him; the day he left for work carrying her sharp words that he should help more with Janak and the housework. How upset had he been by her anger? Had it distracted him? The sense of being complicit in her husband's death dragged her eyes to the edge of the platform. Under a wall, under a train. Would that even things out for you, Ajit? And Janak? She shook herself and stepped back from the edge as the train glided in. She must take control.

Later that morning, she finally raised the concerns about the credit card with Andrew taking more care than usual with her words.

'You're funny, Uma. Sally told me you were an old pedant, worrying too much about the little things. I didn't realise you had such a sense of humour.' Andrew pushed back in his large chair, hands behind his head, and grinned. 'You certainly have worked out my old friend Sally Eling, haven't you?' he laughed. 'Known her from uni. She always knew how to look after Sally. Don't worry about these expenses. Sally will have sorted out how she can claim them.'

Then, as though remembering that he was her manager, he added, 'You're very diligent, Uma, but you need to go easy. You've been looking a bit stressed lately. You're driving staff too hard, I hear. Relax a bit. Just do what needs to be done, don't overdo it.'

Uma's hands began to shake. She clenched her fists. Clouds of migraine were forming like a storm just behind her eyes. She thanked him and left his office.

She'd go for a walk in her lunch break, toss off this murky familiar of depression before it took hold. Along Hunter Street and down Macquarie, admiring the State Library across the street, all the way to Bridge and across to George Street, she pounded along in her thick-soled sneakers, until she turned back into Hunter Street. Something took her eye through the revolving glass doors of the Rockpool Restaurant. Inside, in a passing glance, she saw Sally, Richard and Andrew, heads together over the white-linen covered table, champagne in their glasses. A business lunch? In that instant as Uma paused, Andrew said something that caused Richard and Sally to sit back rolling with laughter. The memory of his recent conversation with her galled her.

Knowing Andrew was still at lunch, Uma called Human Resources. 'Liz. Uma. Can you give me access to a few files—yes, all the division heads. Just checking I've got my figures right.' It wasn't quite a lie. And indeed, something she did need to do from time to time. Nothing Liz would quibble about. Her brain was buzzing with Andrew's conversation and the image from the restaurant scene.

She opened Andrew's HR file. She already knew that there'd been no normal recruitment process. He'd been contracted at short notice to fill Neville's position. She saw now that there was very little in the file at all. A brief letter accepting the invitation from the department head to take on the role. No CV. No references, no indications his proposal had been checked in any way. Just a handwritten note from Sally approving his starting date.

That night, Uma opened the notes she had taken on her mobile phone under a heading 'Concerns: SE'. *Contracts paid out and cancelled with no work done. Regular payment for personal items. Vale contract—not sure???* She added a fourth: *Giving a senior job to a friend.*

Was she overreacting? Was it any of her business? Who cared what Sally did?

Janak and his girlfriend Allison came by on Saturday afternoon. She turned the conversation to the recent embarrassment of a politician.

'What does someone do if they think someone in the office is doing the wrong thing?' she asked. Janak was only half-listening. 'Janak?' she insisted.

'Oh, I don't know, mum, maybe the police? Or the Independent Commission Against Corruption?'

'You're a lawyer, Janak, you should know. Say, a Member of Parliament's Personal Assistant thought there was something wrong. What should they do?'

'Probably get a new job', laughed Janak. 'What do you think, Ali?'

Uma took up Janak's flippant comment and checked the Independent Commission Against Corruption website. It was overloaded with information, too much to take in all at once.

Definitions, procedures, guarantees of confidentiality, principles of integrity, protection for whistle-blowers, and so on. She sat before the ICAC site for the next three nights until her eyes watered with the detail of it. And then there were the reports themselves. Too many to peruse. Too many of them detailing offences that sounded very similar to the things she was observing in her own department.

On Thursday night, tired and confused, she decided to drop the idea of reporting. It was too risky, despite the assurances. What would she be? A whistle-blower? She sensed that whistle-blowers did not have successful careers. She slept dreamlessly, her antidepressants kicking in against her unresolved sense of fairness.

On Friday, Uma felt heavy. Her mind was jumbled. Something about the recent contract awarded to Vale Constructions niggled at her. It had been awarded very quickly—a massive contract for construction of social housing in the inner west of the city, 500 low-cost dwellings, worth $200 million. She waited till Sally was out at lunch and opened the records on the tender and the contract. What was it about this company that troubled her? She scanned the detail. She checked the Australian Securities and Investments Commission website, paying the $19 fee with her personal card. When she saw 'Directors and relationships', she let out a long sigh. A key player in Vale Constructions was Magda Vale. She checked further. It was not hard to follow the line: Magda Vale had two sons, Richard and Mitchell. She was not interested in Mitchell. She couldn't take on more information than she needed, more trouble than she wanted. But Richard. Richard Vale, the boyfriend, partner or, as Steph would say, 'squeeze' of Sally Eling, director of the department awarding the contract.

Uma felt dizzy. Nauseous. She shut the page down. She felt her panic taking over. She grabbed the corners of her desk, shut her eyes.

'Breathe', she told herself, 'Breathe. In, out.' As she'd been taught in the clinic. In. Out.

'Are you okay, Uma?' It was Steph. 'You look as though you've seen me in my undies.'

Uma just nodded, waved a hand to settle her PA.

'I'm okay', she nodded again. 'Bathroom.'

She stood up carefully and walked stiffly to the washroom, getting to the toilet just in time before the bile gushed in vomit. She leaned against the partition, trying to breathe slowly. Flushed. Washed. Rinsed her mouth, just as Steph came in.

She put up both hands to stop the younger woman's question.

When Steph said, 'I think you should go home, Uma', she simply nodded in agreement.

'I'll sign out', she said, 'Get some fresh air.'

Steph stood back to let her leave the washroom. 'Take care, Uma.'

She took two weeks' leave. She spent the first week preparing a notification that she sent to ICAC. All the details. If ICAC chose to investigate her allegations, it could take months. She then checked herself into a health resort for a week.

When she returned to work, wan and edgy, Steph greeted her warmly.

Andrew had left. A better offer had come up. Uma knew there was staff gossip about her own mental condition. She rarely saw Sally.

She carried on her work, occasionally taking notes. Nothing had changed, but she had lost interest in recording the details. She knew she should. She had put all her effort into that initial report to ICAC. She'd done her job. She'd just keep her head down and add up figures and produce reports.

Three months later, Sally initiated a review of the finance division. Uma predicted what might eventuate, but she had no interest in applying elsewhere. She was tired. Unsurprisingly, the review recommended some restructuring: even less surprising to Uma, her position no longer existed. Legal advice suggested she should fight it. Instead, she resigned.

A little later, she heard, Sally too had left, taking up a senior role elsewhere.

The billboard promoting a candidate in the coming state elections cast a diagonal shadow on the pavement. *Vote* SALLY ELING.

A representative you can trust. In the darkness it cast, Uma hadn't noticed the bench in the corner, nor a small figure sitting at one end. She paused, walked back to check. Someone young, huddled in a hoody on the seat, knees up blocking the face, a checked plastic bag and rolled-up sleeping bag clamped under the elbows.

Uma approached slowly, talking softly to herself. She sat down with an exaggerated sigh at the other end of the bench.

'Mind if I share your bench? Just need to rest my feet awhile.' It was a young woman, she realised now, who glanced sideways at Uma and shrugged her shoulders.

'Whatever', she said.

'On my way to work', Uma persisted. 'Going far yourself, love?'

'Dunno', said the girl.

Uma looked at her directly. 'My name's Uma. Some people think it's a name for a grandma, but it's just my name. Can I call you a name?'

'Skye.'

'Skye. That's a lovely name. Skye, love, you look as tired as I feel. I could do with a good cup of tea. It's my birthday and I'd love some company. Breakfast? At Maccas?' She gestured to the golden arches a short way along the street. 'A burger?'

Skye hesitated. She began to gather her belongings.

'Okay, but you gotta pay.'

'Of course', said Uma, 'It's my treat.' She wondered how hungry Skye must be for safe company and warm food.

They sat near the window, Skye constantly watching the street. Uma could see now how pale the girl was, her face spotty, her light brown hair lank. Probably early twenties, about the age Uma was when she was married. The contrast between this young woman and herself as a bride bedecked in jewels, silk sari and manicured hennaed hands disturbed her.

'Got somewhere to stay tonight?' Uma asked casually as she sipped green tea. Skye chewed on a cheeseburger. 'I have some friends—in fact, the place I work—and they'd have a bed for you.' Skye looked up, a little suspiciously. 'You'd be safe, you know.

I can vouch for it. There's staff and it's secure. No one can get in who shouldn't be there.'

Uma could tell Skye was listening. She hadn't said anything; continued eating. Then she wiped her mouth, pushed the cardboard box aside and stood up.

'Okay.'

'Okay', Uma smiled. 'Let's go. It's just a short walk.'

Nothing but the Truth

Sujata Sankranti

The court room was full, as expected. Not a single vacant seat in the gallery. In fact, the crowd had spilled over, snatching every inch of space. Some were squatting on the floor, and some were huddled in the corners. Some leaned on the wall close to the aisle forming unruly lines. What a crowd! People from every walk of life seemed to be here. Were they here to seek justice for the accused? Or even for the victim whom we had already lost? I was sure that it was for neither of these reasons that they thronged to the courthouse. They were the kind who would scan newspapers for sensational stories. For them, a murder, a suicide or a gang rape would be juicy news items to follow. Simply for vicarious pleasure.

There were village folks too. In large numbers. Holding placards, parading their solidarity with the accused, they stood outside the court. Each one of them knew the truth. Yet, here they were, screaming their support for the accused. Facing them, stood another group. Most of them were women, from the Mahila Kalyan Samiti. 'We want justice, justice for Tulsi', they screamed at the top of their voices. They too held banners and placards. *Down down patriarchy. Reeti riwaaz badal daalo.* The slogans, printed in bright red, stood challengingly against the white background of the banners. As announced in the newspapers, they had marched down to the court in a rally. I noticed that a couple of them were helping themselves to cold drinks and snacks. Obviously, refreshing themselves so that they could protest more vociferously. The two groups stood facing each other as though they were in an improvised war zone.

What an uphill task it had been for us to even file the FIR! I must admit that Mrs Kumar, the lady in white who was the Mahila Kalyan Samiti leader, had been very helpful to us. Without her contacts with the police and the higher-ups in the ruling party, it would have been impossible for us to find our way through the muddle of investigation, arrest, trial court, to finally arrive at this juncture—to this day, the D-day, the day of the verdict. But strangely, for some reason, I had begun to feel that somewhere, at some time, the struggle for justice for our dear Tulsi, had been hijacked and turned into a campaign. A motivated campaign. Our loss, our tragedy had now become an issue. If they were to win the case, it would be a feather in their cap. The press and the public would applaud them!

If the battalion of women who were shouting for justice had an agenda, the villagers too had a mission before them. They must prove that Badri Prasad, the accused, was not guilty. Even though many of them were accomplices in the crime and had even helped Badri to erase all the evidence, here they were, projecting him as the victim. He was an unfortunate father who had lost his beloved daughter.

A sharply divided crowd!

But where was Tulsi in this tug of war? If Badri was the victim, what was Tulsi's status?

For Anand and Kamala, his widowed mother, and for me, it was a different story altogether. We sat in the middle row, trying to make ourselves as invisible as we could. Tense and nervous. We had thrown in our lot together to seek justice for our beloved Tulsi, Anand's beautiful bride of barely two months. Murdered by the tyrant of a father to safeguard the honour of his family and the biradari he belonged to. Tulsi could never have taken her own life, as Badri Prasad and the villagers claimed. She had been so full of life, happy, contented. Together, the newly wedded pair had been looking forward to a glorious future. Badri and his extended family of the village might swear and bellow to the world that Tulsi had committed suicide in shame. But we knew the truth of their lie.

Truth chasing lies, lies chasing truth. Was it a game of hide and seek? What a vicious circle! Was there a way out? Was there any hope for us?

There it was, the state emblem of India, staring at me from behind the elevated bench where the honourable judge would soon be seated. The three lions standing back to back amicably and the silver-encrusted inscription below, *Satyameva Jayate*, in Devanagari script, *Truth, nothing but the truth, triumphs...* The court had got everything right, all set to dispense justice.

Badri Prasad who stood in the dock with his arms folded seemed to be looking in the same direction. The hallowed emblem and the statue of the blindfolded goddess of Justice holding the sword and the scale. Permanent fixtures of a ritualistic court.

Do they really uphold truth and assure justice for the victim? Badri's face was hard and inscrutable. Was he handcuffed? Probably not. He was only accused. His innocence or guilt had not been formally proved. When convicted, I hoped against hope, he would not only be handcuffed but also put in chains. After all, he was nothing short of a beast in human form.

When I had first seen Badri in his own village, he had looked as indifferent and stern as he did now. Knowing that he had just returned home after his only daughter's funeral, I had been a bit hesitant in greeting him. But he had folded his palms in a gesture of namaskar and asked me to be seated. Presumably, he thought I had come from the institution where Tulsi had been working. But the moment he spotted Anand by my side, his countenance had changed.

'How dare you come here? You swine! You drove my daughter to this end.'

Anand was shaken. 'What kind of a father are you? How could you do this to your own blood? And you blame me now? I demand an explanation from you. What have you done to my wife?'

'Your wife? I don't know her. Nobody here does.'

'Tulsi came to meet you in all trust, at your request. I am sure of that. I had warned her to be wary of you. To never fall into your trap. Had I been with her that evening, I would have stopped her from coming to you.'

Badri's face had turned red and blue. No sorrow, no shame. Only fury glinted in his eyes. Behind him a crowd had already gathered. The village headman, the elders and the neighbours. They turned to Anand. 'How dare you come to our village? You have brought shame and dishonour to our village. If you care for your life, better get away from here.'

'I don't care about my life. Not anymore. Kill me as you have done with my wife.'

'She took her life because you forced her into an unholy relationship.'

'That is a lie. She has been my wedded wife for the last two months. And we were the happiest souls on the earth. But tell me, how did you lure her here? Nothing is straight and fair with you, I have always known that. And I did tell her so. But my poor Tulsi, she was so naive, so innocent!'

I had to plead with Anand not to aggravate the situation. With great difficulty I persuaded him to retreat. The only thing we could do now was to register a case against Badri Prasad.

It took a week for us to file the FIR accusing Badri for the coldblooded, premeditated murder of his own daughter. In all probability, in the presence of other family members. But all of them, the mute witnesses of the diabolic act, chose to defend Badri. Dutifully.

And now, we were here, all of us, waiting for the crucial verdict. The judge would walk in ceremoniously. At any moment. And would occupy that lofty seat behind which were displayed the words *Truth, nothing but the truth, triumphs.*

Anand sat like a statue by my side. Silent, with a fixed faraway look in his eyes.

'Come on Anand, let's hope for the best. God is great.' I tried to pull him out of his reverie. But he just kept looking at me with blank eyes. Poor boy! How thin and pale he looked! I addressed him these days as an old young man. He must be around twenty-six or twenty-seven. But the prolonged course of court proceedings, the endless sessions of interrogations, hearings and trials, the war of words between the defence counsel and the prosecutor... the ordeal had added years to his face.

When he had first come to meet me at my home, he had been an energetic, excited young man. 'I came to know about you through a friend of mine. He said that you had helped him to get his father's pension restored. I am sure you can help me too. I need your advice.'

'But young man, I am not a professional counsellor. I do help people when they have genuine problems. I am not attached to any institution.'

'Yes didi, that is all the more reason why I have come to you. I don't know how to deal with formalities. This is Tulsi', he said fondly, pointing at the girl who had come with him. A petite pale-complexioned girl, probably in her late teens.

'Yes, what can I do for you both?'

'Didi, we want to get married.'

'Go and tell your families. Simple enough.'

'Oh! That is exactly the problem. Her family is dead against it.'

'Why?'

'Her father wouldn't hear of such a match, because', and he paused significantly, 'I belong to a lower caste.'

'Caste?'

'Yes didi. Intercaste marriages are not allowed in their biradari. And a lower-caste groom? It's unthinkable.'

'If you love each other and trust each other, no one can stop you, my dear.'

'Didi, it is not that simple. Her father is a tyrant. If Tulsi defies his orders, he can go to any extent to stop her.'

'So, what do you want me to do? Go to her parents and plead with them?'

'No, we just want to get married. How do we go about it?'

'How old are you?'

'I am twenty-three and Tulsi is nineteen.

'Well, you are both adults. Go and get married in the court. Or go to a temple; the priest will get you married and give you a certificate.'

'But we are afraid. I told you, her father is a vindictive man and he may try to harm us.'

'You can get police protection. That's if you can convince the authorities that there is genuine threat to your life.'

'Please, didi, you must help us in this matter. We will be grateful to you forever.'

The couple looked at me pleadingly and I didn't have the heart to disappoint them. I couldn't attend their marriage ceremony though, which was held in an Arya Samaj temple. But after a week or so they came to me with a big box of sweets wrapped in glossy golden sheets and presented me with their wedding photo.

'Oh! A souvenir for me?' I laughed.

It was a lovely photo. The garlanded beaming couple, a bouquet each in their hands, stood posing in front of the Taj Mahal.

'Oh! Did you go to Agra for your honeymoon?'

'No, no. How could we ever think of moving out of the city? Her family is on the watch out. The studio had all sorts of backdrops to choose from, didi. From Niagara Falls to Eiffel Tower. Tulsi chose the Taj Mahal because it is the symbol of love.'

'Of eternal love', Tulsi chipped in with a smile.

Hardly three months had passed. Anand appeared again at my door. This time, minus Tulsi. He was ashen-faced. Blood-shot eyes and crumpled clothes. Obviously, he had spent a sleepless night. The moment he saw me, he broke down into sobs. 'Didi, Tulsi has gone.'

'Where to?'

'I wish I knew. She has been missing since the day before evening. She had gone to buy vegetables from a nearby mundi.'

'Where was the policeman guarding your house?'

'He said he had followed her and had been watching her from a nearby tea shop. She had been selecting vegetables. All of a sudden, she disappeared from his view. He says he waited for an hour and when she didn't turn up he came home to inform me.'

'Didn't you make a complaint at the police station?'

'I did. But no news so far. I am sure her family has kidnapped her.'

'Didn't you call her on her mobile?'

'I did. But it's switched off.'

Anand broke down again.

'Let's wait for a day. Maybe the police will find some clues.'

Anand shook his head without much conviction.

The next day I received a frantic phone call from Anand. 'She's gone, didi, gone forever. My two-month-old bride is no more!' He sobbed into the phone.

Tulsi's school friend and neighbour, Veena, had called him and given him the shocking news. Tulsi's mother had told Veena that her daughter was coming home to offer prayers in the local Kali temple. Newly married women always performed a puja in this shrine to seek the blessings of Kali for their suhag. It was a traditional ritual of their community. But Veena said that when she went to the temple to meet her, she wasn't there. The priest said neither Tulsi, nor anyone from her house had come to offer prayers. Late that night, she and her parents had heard shouts and screams from Tulsi's house. But they decided not to venture out, fearing for their own safety. Next morning, to their horror, they found Tulsi hanging on the branches of the mango tree in their backyard.

'Hey bhagwaan! How can I bear it? You should have taken me, not my innocent daughter', the mother grieved, thumping her chest. 'How can I bear to see her like this? Hanging on the tree that had given her her favourite fruit, year after year. That rogue lured my daughter with gifts and promises and then abandoned her. She was so depressed, my poor daughter! I curse him, that villain. May he never know peace.'

Tulsi had been betrayed. There was no doubt. But by whom? By her husband, or by her family? Veena said she had her doubts. But no one asked her or her family anything.

'The father', she said, 'sat like a stone without a trace of feeling and silently watched Tulsi's brother light the pyre.'

Of course, there was an enquiry and a post-mortem before the body was consigned to flames. The doctor certified that Tulsi had died of asphyxia as normally found in most suicide cases by hanging.

Later, the junior doctor who was present at the post-mortem told Anand that there were bruises on her neck and upper arms, suggesting a struggle. On our request, he testified in court about his suspicions. So did Veena, about the deadly screams that had broken the silence of that black ominous night. But unfortunately, they reversed their accounts after the initial witness hearing. It was obvious that the elders of the village and the members of the community court had silenced them!

Reversals and denials! It was shocking! Outrageous! The defence lawyer had been bought with money power. The witnesses who were initially loyal to us had been bullied and scared away. Justice for poor Tulsi seemed to be wishful thinking now. Yet, we waited—Anand, Kamala and I—for the words from the horse's mouth.

The echo of a gong woke me up rudely from my daze.

Bell, book and candle?

The judge read out in a dispassionate, oratorical tone... 'In the absence of crucial circumstantial evidence, the accused is...'

My god! Acquitted... Badri Prasad is acquitted! This was like a Bollywood climax... as unbelievable, as unwarranted.

The crowd heaved out of the room. I didn't care to look at them. Who cheered, who condemned did not matter to us. I put my arms around Anand.

'It's not over Anand. We have not lost. We will appeal to the higher court. What if we don't have witnesses? We will request polygraph tests...'

From the far end of the room, I heard someone guffawing.

'A lie detector? When I placed my hand on the sacred Bhagavad Gita to take my oath, my hand did not shake. When I looked straight in the eyes of the three lions and repeated "I will speak nothing but truth", my voice didn't break. If I can quash my conscience, the god within me, what can a machine do?'

But who was this incorrigible, callous creature having the last laugh?

I rushed forward to silence him... But there was nobody at the other end. All I could see was the dwarfed shadow of the giant banyan tree across the road. Swaying in the hot afternoon breeze.

Smokescreen

A Room Made of Leaves

Kate Grenville

One evening, a year after the night of *four thousand pounds*, Mr Macarthur unveiled another grand scheme.

—My dearest, he said as we sat down by the fire after dinner, it has been evident to me for some time that we have had the best of what speculation can offer. I have deliberated on our future here, and see that the way forward is in the production of fine wool.

—Of fine wool! I said, and only someone who knew me better than Mr Macarthur would have heard my astonished amusement.

—A thinking man has always been able to see that this colony needs a product fit for export, he said. Wool fits the bill. We have proved how well sheep can do in this country.

I held up my fan as if to shield my cheeks from the fire.

—My Spanish purchases have shown what is possible, he said. The scheme of putting the Spanish to inferior crosses has exceeded all my hopes.

From behind the fan I watched him. He betrayed not the slightest awareness that the scheme, as he called it, was nothing he had ever intended. He was not pretending, not lying. I saw that his greatest strength was to enter so fully into his constructions that he authentically forgot they were not true.

He strode about the room talking with such passion that white spittle gathered at the corners of his mouth. Not only had he put the sheep together in such a way as to produce the finest wool the world had ever seen. He would go further, and take into his own hands every aspect of bringing it to market.

Editors' note: This extract from the novel *A Room Made of Leaves*, set in the earliest days of Sydney, reminds us of the persuasive allure of false narratives as Grenville imagines the secret life of Elizabeth Macarthur.

You could not simply put casks of John Macarthur wool on a ship and send them to London and expect the wool merchants to flock down to the wharf demanding it! A knowledgeable fellow would have to be there, someone with a nose for a deal who could be trusted to see the business through. There was only one man who was fit for the task: himself. As soon as he could, he would find a pretext to get leave of absence from the Corps and take a passage to London with a shipment of wool. He apologised that I would be obliged to stay in New South Wales. Laid the flattery on thick.

—I am perfectly aware, my dear wife, of the difficulties you will encounter in looking after our interests here, he said. I am fully convinced that not one in a thousand would have the resolution and perseverance to contend with them. But I have confidence in you, my dearest wife, to surmount them in a way that will make me grateful and delighted.

I had to pretend to doubt my ability. It would not do to look eager. But it was not difficult to strike the right note, because he was hardly listening. His horizon was filled with the picture of himself striding the stage of London, a new-world Jason dazzling all before him with his golden fleece. The more difficult feat was not allowing him to glimpse my relief.

Six months to sail to England. Six months back again. A year in between to get his nose into those deals. Two years, then. And if Hannaford and I could continue to send one shipment after the other, Mr Macarthur might feel obliged to stay in London to sell those too. The challenge—my mind, like his, was flying over the future—would be to make sure that the flow of wool was good, but never so good that it would furnish enough capital for us to return to England. I let myself imagine it: two years, four years. Eight years.

But told myself not to hope. He was not gone yet.

There was a beautiful logic to it all. Mr Macarthur wanted to trade wool. I was content to be left behind to produce it. It gave me wry satisfaction to understand that in this business, if in no other, Mr Macarthur and I fitted together as sweetly as a dovetail joint.

* * *

Mr Macarthur left Parramatta on the packet boat to Sydney on a fine November afternoon. The following day, he would board His Majesty's ship the *Hunter* and sail out of Sydney Cove, past the bays and headlands of the harbour, between the cliffs that the *Scarborough* had brought us through twelve years before, and onto the ocean that would take him to England.

I watched the little boat head off with the tide down the river, take the wide bend where the mangroves spread out into the stream, and disappear. First it was there, then it disappeared as if smoothly swallowed by the mangroves: bow, body, stern, the last flap of the flag hanging behind. I stood watching as if it might appear again, grow larger, return to the dock, as if the whole idea of Mr Macarthur leaving was a delicious fantasy.

I watched for some unmeasured stretch of time, of the new time that belonged to me. Then there were only the dancing points of light on the river, the busy lap of water against the stones of the jetty, a gull sweeping past with one hard sharp cry, and myself, a woman breathing the sweet air of solitude.

* * *

Forty years have passed between then and now, as I sit in the sunny little room in the house at Parramatta where for so long I attended to business. Mr Macarthur called this place Elizabeth Farm, but at the top of my letters it is simply *Parramatta*, and I never write the word without thinking of the people whose language it is, for whom Parramatta has always been, and always will be, the Place of Eels.

Now, after so many years here, I know better than ever what has been done to the Gadigal, the Wangal, the Cameraygal, the Burramattagal and all the others. Not just the turning-off from their lands and the damage to their old ways. Not just the cruelties inflicted. Not just the deaths. Behind all that is another, fundamental violence: the replacement of the true history by a false one.

Closest to home—literally, as I sit here looking down towards the river where the event is supposed to have taken place—is what happened an hour after dawn on that summer morning when Pemulwuy threw a spear at a soldier.

He escaped from the hospital, the fetter still around his leg. He led another few years of *depredations* till at last a reward was offered for him to be caught, dead or alive. A settler shot him, and to prove the fact cut off his head, which was sent to England for the scientific gentlemen.

The death of one man did not mean the end of attacks: they continue to this day in the distant parts. How could it be otherwise? *Depredations and outrages* are our words. Another way to describe what is going on is to call it *defending a homeland*.

But after that morning the settlers felt a new confidence. They called the affray The Battle of Parramatta, as if those few minutes of hubbub could take their place beside the battles of Thermopylae or Agincourt, a victory that signalled God's approval.

The Battle of Parramatta confirms the story the settlers tell themselves about the people they displaced: that they are irrational and lack good sense. Heavens, they thought they could take on one of His Majesty's fortified garrisons! The story, and all the others like it, convinces the settlers that, in dispossessing the first inhabitants, they are simply part of the natural order, in which the strong and clever replace the weak and foolish. It might be sad, but they assure each other that it is as inevitable as night following day.

Mr Macarthur wrote an account of the affray, which must have been sent to the governor, who must have relayed it to Captain Collins, who was at that time in England. Collins used it in his account of the colony, and as far as I know it has never been questioned.

Perhaps it was my lessons in astronomy that make me doubt what seems beyond doubt. That, and my knowledge that Pemulwuy's people are neither weak nor foolish. The story relayed by Captain Collins is really only credible if you believe they are.

I cannot tell you just what happened on that far-off morning. I only know that it could not have been as Mr Macarthur told it to me, and as Captain Collins has told the world. Knowing my husband as I do, I have no doubt that it was some tale of trickery: a trap or an ambush or a promise betrayed. Whatever it is, the truth has been silenced, and this other story put in its place.

I am a newcomer here, ignorant of the inner grain of the place. The lifetime of one woman cannot be put beside the uncountable generations of the people who were here before me. Still, newcomer though I am, this is home to me now. Any other place would be exile.

I understand, though, that mon petit coin, that room made of leaves down by the river, is not really à moi. Like most of the other newcomers, in the past I never gave a proper name to what I was doing. Now I am prepared to be more honest. As Mrs Brown did, I have to face the fact that I am a thief. More a thief than Mrs Brown, who was a thief only once. I have been a thief for every one of those forty years.

Yes, I make sure the people who live within our boundaries are treated well. I supply them with various items that they seem to value, although they lived without them until recently and, after all, it is because of our coming that they need them now. We greet each other by name, and we converse a little—in English, since their English is so much better than my Burramattagal—about this and that, like any other neighbours.

But underneath that goodwill, we all know an undigestible fact: I am not prepared to give them back what has always been theirs. Not prepared to gather up my children and get on a ship and return to the place of our forebears.

I can see no way to put right all the wrongs done, no more than I could all those years ago when I picked up the stick belonging to a Burramattagal woman and heard what it was saying. The difference is that now I do not turn away. I am prepared to look in the eye what we have done.

That repairs no part of the sorrow of it, I know. But it is the first thing, the first hard truth, without which no repair can ever be hoped for.

Outside the window the last glow of the day lies softly on the garden, and beyond are the big calm trees that have been growing for so many years, long before Elizabeth Veale took up space in the world. What comfort there is in knowing that trees, sunlight, birds go on, indifferent to the life in this house, or in the heart of the woman at its heart.

What I see now is that destiny, Providence—whatever name you might give to bald luck—gave me two glorious stretches of time without Mr Macarthur. His first absence was four years, the second closer to a decade. When he returned the second time, the alternating bouts of mania and black gloom had taken over his life. He was like a machine that runs too fast and smokes and creaks till it tears itself to pieces. What a glorious irony that his madness in the end took the form of a conviction that his wife was being unfaithful to him. Many years after his wife had revelled in the embraces of Mr Dawes, Mr Macarthur spoke the truth, but by then he had been too mad for too long, had made too many accusations, and no one listened.

The years of his absence presented me with chances offered to few women. Managing the flocks without him, I was not wife, not widow, not old maid. None of those, yet all of them at once. In the ambiguity of my situation I could be nothing more or less than myself, and to be what we all are, especially at the end: alone.

What an unsung pleasure it is to be alone when we are supposed to fear it. Dull it might seem, but as a woman who has survived an interesting marriage, I am happy to be dull.

Now, in what I suppose a poet might call the *evening of my life*, it is the evenings I love best. At the end of the day it is like a prayer to walk down to the river when the shadows are lying long over the grass. Every evening there is lovely, but today a storm had recently passed, and in the orange glow of sunset a tremendous sky laid itself out like a vast noble text. There was every kind of cloud: crisp white flecks stippled in loose lines, white wisps like an old man's hair, dramatic piles laid thick as carpet, pink puffs catching an edge of sunset, and, as if wandered in from another sky altogether, two small bright clouds exactly the shape of Mr Dawes's lenses.

I sat on the log watching the light fade, the river holding the soft glow of the sky. There were five Burramattagal children picking their way along a slip of sand, each child's long thin legs straightening and jointing, straightening and jointing, legs made for walking great distances, never tiring, and every jointing, every straightening, reflected with absolute fidelity in the water at their feet so it seemed there were ten children, five upside down and five the right way up. Each seemed as real as the other, so you could wonder which was child, which reflection. Which the eternal past of this place, and which the eternal future, those feet part of the land through all time.

I write this—why? What does it matter that those children made a thing of such beauty that I felt compelled to record it? What does it matter that there was a person the future will remember as Elizabeth Macarthur, who wanted to be known for who she was?

I will give this private account no title. I see it as a river like the one I grew up beside, always curling on, dimpling and surging in its bed, never fixed and measurable but only ever a moment—There! That!—giving way to another moment—That! There!

Mr Dawes would say: Write nothing. Leave nothing. What do you care if people in the future believe the insipid fiction of your letters? He would be right. In the unimaginable future when these papers are found, no one will remember Mrs Macarthur, and her glorious husband will be nothing more than a dim name in a dull book about the past.

Mr Dawes would be right, but he would be wrong, too. I am no poet, but like them I am greedy to be remembered, even by some stranger of the future, as one true person, speaking straight into the face of time. Others want to find God. I have always had a more modest aim. I am happy enough to find myself coming to meet myself in what I have written here, and stand up in greeting.

There is a bush down by the river that in this season is hung with a thousand seed pods, each one twisted like a question mark. They dance silvery pale among the dark leaves, the whole bush laughing, it seems, trembling in the breeze, the fine leaves and the tiny curved pods asking their question. I stop as I pass, and smile as if at an old friend.

And in a way it is an old friend, because when I see it I think of Mr Dawes. He would have enjoyed the question-mark bush. I can imagine him saying, *If we wait long enough, Mrs Macarthur, the entire sentence may be revealed to us.*

Well, Mr Dawes, I would like to hear that sentence. And I am ready to wait.

Blanket

Priya Sarukkai Chabria

I will answer your question:

On the day of a child's birth, the State gifts the baby a blanket which it wears for the rest of its life. Each blanket comes with the newborn's name embossed.

Educational institutions which the child enters, beginning with playschool, gift the child a blanket on the first day. Colleges and other institutions of higher education follow suit, as do polytechnics. Dropouts too are awarded fitting blankets emblazoned with the words 'Dropout from school/college/PhD' or at whichever level of education the citizen stopped studying, thus attempting to thwart the State's plan for their future.

Corporate houses, the power and industrial sectors (that harvest the Earth's resources for maximum benefit to all) too gift a blanket to every new recruit, irrespective of gender, caste or creed, but in accordance with each one's rank. Each promotion means the person is gifted another blanket that is deemed suitable for their new position. Similarly, on retirement, each person is gifted yet another blanket, of a synthetic aurous hue as a parting gift. This system of handing out blankets is similarly followed by the numerous guilds of commerce. Underworld dons impose strict rules of blanket gifting and wearing on their underlings. Needless to add, the armed forces are given blankets by the State, as are public sector employees. Even in the unorganised sector, people are given blankets appropriate to their station in life, which they wear every day until they too retire and are given replacement blankets of the coarsest recycled material, which, however, covers them completely. The State does not overlook the unemployed either; each one is provided one under the Improved Blanket Scheme for the Jobless. Thus all citizens wear blankets which signify their standing in society.

Politicians wear hypnotic blankets of changing rainbow hues; those of bureaucrats, minions, social media influencers and media personnel down to the lowest rung wear blankets that chameleon-like mimic the colours of their masters' blankets. These, presented to them by their overlords of the season, are, naturally, of a reduced order of glitter.

Couples gift each other blankets when their relationship turns serious; for the passing pleasures of single nights or weekend romances, the couple gift each other coverlets. As part of their wedding vows, newlyweds gift each other blankets which once again are apt for the intensity of their love or indicative of the comfort level expected in their arranged marriages. When couples become parents, they gift each other new blankets and two tiny blankets for their newborn, one each from father and mother. It is unnecessary to add that divorcees, widowers and widows also receive blankets befitting their new identities, as do couples in live-in relationships which are terminated by mutual consent or otherwise. A special category of threadbare blankets is reserved for aged former first wives who are dumped by their husbands in favour of younger women. Nary a person is without blankets during any stage of their private or public lives.

In this way people accumulate blankets which they use daily, wearing one on top of another and adding the ones which reflect their current status in life. This means that by the time a person dies, each has accumulated a pile of blankets which are then buried or burnt with them as per their religion.

You pose too many questions. Let me recap.

First, don't the people feel hot wearing layers of blankets one over the other? Second, how can they move about freely? Thirdly, surely at some point they want to kick off their blankets—for after all, everyone does.

Patience. I will answer each one. It is clear that you have not understood our system. I will elaborate. Listen:

The earlier ones thin into a whisper of air when covered by the freshest blanket. The blankets also grow in size; they wrap themselves just so, over their owners, snugly, like a second skin, so much so that people do not realise they are enveloped by a sheath of blankets all the time. People talk through the blankets, make love through them, eat, shit, bathe and perform all functions, bodily and otherwise, through them, without the slightest discomfort. The blankets rise and fall, mimicking their breathing, every single inhalation and every single exhalation, to perfection.

As for your third question, here is my answer:

Blankets provide the people comfort. In truth, they are security blankets which grow thread-like filaments that dig like millions of root hairs into the owners' bodies so that when the person attempts to shrug off a blanket, she or he experiences extreme stress and discomfort.

The few who, for whatever reason, attempt to rip off a layer or two of their blankets, find themselves in the wards of mental hospitals where kindly doctors and nurses help them garb themselves correctly again.

A moment, please. Let me explain the process.

First, they are cajoled to slip on the soft, ameliorating blanket of never questioning what they see, read or hear, never to resist what they are told about the world or their happy situation in it. Next, they are seduced into accepting the silky blanket of good behaviour. This is followed by the gift of the fluffiest 'Welcome Back' blanket which allows them to be re-accepted by their peers and loved ones, return to their jobs and regain their social status; they are once again invited to parties and always win the first hand at rummy.

Incorrect!

The news item you refer to that some people try to tear off their blankets is a fabrication perpetrated by confused rabble-rousers, egged on by a hostile foreign press. Such 'dissenters'—you will notice I adopt your choice of word—are quickly enlightened. They run back to the cosiness of their blankets that guide them through routine and rigour, playtime and professional deportment, pleasure and pain; verily, through any issue which might occasionally present itself to them.

You are persistent. However, I will answer this query as well as we have nothing to hide.

If such reports are to be believed, minor disturbances may manifest via songs, supposedly heard by the victim. Apparently irresistible, the effect is purported to be much like that of a siren song, which takes control of their minds. Nevertheless, myth has warned us of the fate that befalls those lured by sirens. Besides, warnings are regularly broadcast to keep the populace vigilant about said mishaps. It is also recommended they immediately inform authorities if they become susceptible to 'siren song' influence.

No, there is no question of your implied doubt becoming fact.

I am Chief of Blanket Distribution, Sector 14/54/G, so heed my authority when I say that no one is told how to behave or what to believe. They are free and independent-minded citizens of an advanced democratic society which is spreading over the entire world. People know everything they receive is pure and genuine: every sensation, word and image, every thought and feeling; assuredly, every experience they had, have and will have is true. Like the mesmerising displays of sunsets, rainbows and moonlight that we daily see on our screens.

This is why no one wants to live without their blankets. Nor should anyone attempt otherwise.

I trust your misgivings are now laid to rest. Let us end this interview with you observing my example. Notice my glossy, coveted pelt, gathered over decades.

What? Why do I scratch? It's a rash, a passing rash. Ignore it.

The Verdict

Andrew Kwong

'... the young girl's death was a result of the viral infection caused by meningococcal meningitis... the teenager's death was a preventable one by her GP, should he take...'

The coroner's final verdict hit like a bullet that pierced through Dr Martin Assef's heart.

For many years now, the fresh face of the bright teenager who died during an epidemic of the flu still flashed in front of him, often when he was on his way to work at his general practice.

'Caring for the local community'—a proud mission statement on the sign outside the surgery upheld his belief and commitment to his patients, but it had lost some of its shine since the unexpected death of Cassie.

Cassie moved into town with her single mother Nina one summer and appointed Dr Martin, as he was known by the locals, as their family doctor. She was sixteen years old, the same age as his daughter, and was inquisitive and intelligent. She attended a well-known selective high school in the city some two hours away by train and bus; his daughter at another. Although they never met, Cassie often enquired about his daughter and her studies, with a hint of competitiveness and envy. Sometimes she came in for advice that a daughter would seek from her father, besides the usual colds and minor complaints. Her mother was an ambitious woman navigating her corporate career, but was as caring as any good mother. Her long hours away from home left Cassie by herself most of the day, without a father on the scene.

With sorrow, Dr Martin vividly recalled one Friday afternoon in July many years ago when she had consulted him—the year after Cassie had finished her Higher School Certificate with top marks. Notably unwell, she could hardly manage to get down the steps that led to the surgery. She was pale and had lost the sparkle in her inquiring eyes. She was weak but coherent. A full physical examination confirmed a dehydrated eighteen-year-old recovering from the flu. Before seeing Dr Martin, she had been to the local emergency department twice, visited a GP in Sydney and another two GPs in a nearby medical centre, over a period of ten days. No other threatening signs presented. Dr Martin felt she needed some urgent intravenous fluids in hospital to help recovery. He rang her mother at work and urged her to come home as soon as possible to take her back to the ED.

'They pissed me off last time', Cassie complained, overhearing the conversation, and raised her heavy eyelids, 'I am not going back there.'

Instead she agreed to go to a local private hospital for rehydration, perhaps even further investigation.

At 6 PM, Dr Martin arrived at the private hospital to supervise Cassie's treatment, hoping a couple of litres of intravenous fluids would revitalise her. He planned to discharge her into her mother's care early on Saturday morning, before leaving for the airport for an interstate conference.

'Code blue, ward three. Code blue, ward three.' Out of the loudspeakers came the urgent call as Dr Martin was climbing the stairs to the second level where Cassie was admitted.

'Your patient', the charge nurse cried out as she was rushing the oxygen cylinder into Room 214.

'What happened?' He ran after her.

'She's had less than half a bag of IV fluids, not even 500 ml, and she can't breathe.' The charge nurse already had the mask on Cassie, and oxygen was now flowing at full speed.

'Call the intensivist', Dr Martin ordered, wasting no time as he went over Cassie for clues. She was pale, but puffing at forty breaths per minute. Her heart rate had increased to 110 beats per minute, regular. She was responsive to verbal orders. Her face was turning pink with oxygen.

'BP 78 over 45, temp 36', the other nurse called out loud.

Cassie opened her eyes and was pleased that her GP was there.

'Dr Connell has left', another nurse sang out as she ran back into Room 214.

'Ring his mobile phone, bring him back. Now', Dr Martin cried out. At the same time, he was somewhat relieved that her heart sounds were normal, so was her chest. He double-checked the bases of her lungs to make sure no crepitus was present—a sign of fluid overload or heart failure; no puffy ankles, no abdominal tenderness, no skin eruption or rash, no neck stiffness, and no abnormal neurological signs, reaffirming his earlier examination back at the surgery. But she was as limp as a rag doll.

'Pupils round and responsive to light', the charge nurse reported.

'Raise the end of the bed', Dr Martin said. 'Let's put her into an intensive care unit for the night. Sister, please chase up the blood tests done on admission... And nurse, did you get hold of Dr Connell?'

'You'll be fine, Cassie', he held her hand. 'You'll go home tomorrow morning; by then you'll feel a lot better.'

Cassie nodded, then closed her eyes again.

At the ICU, Dr Connell was not impressed. 'So much for my early night of the week', he mumbled behind the mask that sheltered his own flu he was recovering from. He checked over Cassie, while at the same time discussing with Dr Martin the whole presentation and clinical findings. Speedy action was vital in an emergency, and one had to multitask.

'It's weird! No fever, no abnormal neurological signs, no clinical heart failure, in a young, otherwise healthy girl recovering from the flu. Yet she is so limp', he said.

'All appropriate tests are normal', the charge nurse sang out.

'Here you are nurse, for urgent blood culture please', Dr Connell said as he handed the ICU nurse the tubes of blood he had collected.

'Martin, this is very odd. I don't like it. Let's intubate her and transfer her over to the major hospital where there are more staff and facilities, as well as ICU specialists and doctors on duty.' His earlier annoyance vanished, and his cough didn't seem to bother him. He was most concerned.

'Cassie, we are going to put a tube into your throat to help you breathe easier, and take you over to the public hospital', Dr Connell explained. She lifted her heavy eyelids once more and looked at Dr Martin.

'It's okay, Cassie', said Dr Martin, still holding her hand, 'I'll be there to see you in the morning.'

She shut her eyes.

On Saturday at 6 AM, the ICU specialist at the public hospital said on the phone, 'I'm afraid Cassie is not doing well. She went into cascade organ failure in the night, a phenomenon we often see in the flu victims. We had to resuscitate her several times, but she's now unresponsive. Brain dead. We'll meet with her mother later in the morning to discuss further plan and action. I'm afraid the prognosis is grave.' The specialist, exhausted and notably deflated, tried to sound calm. Dr Martin shared her pain, and was equally baffled by the rapid demise of Cassie, whom he cared so much about.

Cassie died the same afternoon, after Nina agreed to have the respirator turned off.

Looking meticulously for clues, the newly arrived young pathologist felt compelled to report the sighting of two unpaired gram-negative cocci among the many tissue samples. He suspected the dreaded meningococcal infection was the culprit. Later, at the coroner's hearing, evidence of flu from infection experts including a professor of infectious diseases was dismissed as the cause for Cassie's death.

Neisseria meningitidis, the bacterium that causes meningococcal infection, often carries a high mortality rate even in modern times, and it usually claims its victims in a matter of hours, but rarely drags on for days. It has a unique appearance in a paired fashion under the microscope. Post-mortem is not a sterile procedure. Contamination happens as nearly twenty per cent of healthy people carry the germ in their nostrils and hands. Deep down, Dr Martin still believed that she had died from the flu, although it's a rare event for her age group. The eleven-day duration for such a virulent infection had never been reported in published medical literature. How could the coroner's verdict be correct?

Could six doctors who saw Cassie and prescribed no antibiotics for what they thought was the flu have been wrong in the first place? Without the usual meningococcal symptoms apart from lethargy, how did it fit the diagnosis of meningitis? How did it fit with the negative blood and other tissue cultures, with the absence of gram-negative diplococci in brain tissues and body fluids at autopsy? Meningococcal infection, a *virus*, was reported by the town's clerk of the courthouse, who happened to be the newly promoted town coroner. Preventable death by the GP, who was the last doctor to see her and admit her to hospital.

Time passed, but the memory of the tragedy did not fade. Dr Martin recalled the words of the reassuring young lawyer appointed by the medical mutual company when they were about to attend the coroner's court hearing. 'Don't worry', he said, as he munched on his hamburger. 'This is my first coroner's court hearing also. We'll go in and bat, you know, as in cricket', he explained, as if Dr Martin had just arrived from another country.

Dr Martin remembered looking at him, wanting to tell him that he went to school in the country he had adopted, and had played lots of cricket. Instead, he took a long sip of his bottled water.

There was a weird feeling of relief after all the weeks of distress, as the party left the local courthouse after the hearing. Even though Dr Martin was upset by some of the unusual questions put forward by the lawyer from a litigation firm appointed by Cassie's mother. Perhaps it was a form of debriefing in the coroner's court to ease some of the horrible angst and pains for all the parties involved in Cassie's final care. After all, having provided all the information as it happened, Dr Martin thought he had batted well.

Peer review medical journals and professional weekly magazines rushed to report the most unusual meningococcal case to raise awareness among the medical fraternity, and doubted the conclusions by the coroner. Discussions raged among doctors who were obviously bewildered, if not angry, by the erroneous judicial findings. The high-profile case was presented in many hospital grand rounds for all to learn from.

Every doctor dreads the thought of having to face the medical board tribunal to explain their action in caring for their patients. The town coroner dutifully recommended that it should be the case for the last doctor who handled the case. After many months of soul searching and deliberation as Dr Martin waited, the day finally arrived. He decided to catch a train to Sydney to face the tribunal, for fear of not being able to drive home after the appearance, should they rule against his professional integrity.

Two eminent professors of medicine and a senior GP sat at the tribunal. After twenty minutes of agonising wait, as Dr Martin made his appearance, they shook their heads and told him to go home and to continue practising the good medicine he had always been doing. It was obvious they had already examined the big pile of papers on their desk, and seen the questionable judicial report.

Dr Martin wept without shame.

At the local hospital's annual general meeting the following year, the town coroner was invited as the guest speaker.

'For his flawed verdicts of the case, Martin, and passing the buck for you to carry, sparing the district hospital', whispered Dr Connell to Dr Martin with obvious cynicism and distaste. 'Let me explain. The hospital's insurers are commercially orientated and are always prompt to deflect their liability to someone else involved. You know Martin, by so doing they fall into those ambulance-chasing lawyers' clever tactics of making money out of tragedies.'

With his notable experiences in medico-legal matters, Dr Connell's words were credible. 'I was most annoyed with this coroner when he declined my offer to come to give evidence in Cassie's coronial inquiry. Fancy reporting it as a *viral* infection! And the dubious evidence of meningococcal illness.' He continued, 'Besides, if it were true that she did die from that nasty germ, the hospital should be responsible for her initial attendances. Missed opportunities there, twice! Ah, it's all too political when public institutions are challenged. In medicine, they need a face attached to the case to deflect their own responsibilities. So sorry my friend, you were it.' With this, he got up and left the annual general meeting as the speech began.

'Every lawyer gets at least one case in his lifetime that affects him personally.' Atticus's cry in *To Kill a Mockingbird* resonated in Dr Martin. 'So do doctors', he sighed, and nodded to himself. He too, got up, and left the meeting.

Wrong Number

Mitra Phukan

As always, the first thing she did on awakening was to grope around the bed. Her eyes were still closed, but it was as though her fingers had vision. She felt around the narrow bamboo platform, up near her head, and then down towards her waist. She slid her palm over the bed sheet, and felt the small, hard rectangle entangled in there. Slowly, she drew it out, and grasped it. Firmly. It was only then that she opened her eyes.

Today was the day, she thought, looking at the light coming in through the small window on the wall woven with split bamboo. Today, finally. She smiled, and examined the object that she held.

A small red phone. Not a touchscreen or a smartphone. This was a basic model from a little-known company. But she could make and receive calls on it, and also texts. There were a few other things it could do too, but she did not know how to make them work for her. After all, she had studied only up to class three, in a tumbledown shack of a village school. Classes had not been held at all during the four months of the rainy season because the school premises would be waist-deep in water from the Brahmaputra, which would burst its banks every year and come and inundate their village. They would have to shift to the embankment, and take shelter in the tented accommodation that the government set up for them.

That was how it was, every year, for as long as Maini could remember. Nothing changed here, in this small village. She had had to leave off studying, like others, when the school hut had been completely washed away once. That had been many years ago. The place had been put together again, but it was decided at home that there was no point in Maini going to school. Better that she helped her mother around the house, and learned to work the fields as a hired hand, during the season.

No, nothing changed. Nothing, except for… she smiled, and held the little phone a little tighter in her fist… except this little gadget. And though the river still flooded the village every year, with this, her life, and that of many others she knew, had changed. In small ways and big, it had brought change.

She had bought this phone on one of her visits to her uncle's place in the town. She had had it for just about six months now, though she had been saving for it for over a year. She had bought it with the money she got selling the gamosas and sadors she wove on the loom. The payments in cash and kind that she got from the owners of the fields she worked in were handed over to her mother to help run the house. She kept only a little of the cash for herself. For there were expenses. Deuta was getting weaker every winter. Those medicines cost money. And ma needed things that required cash to purchase.

Yes, she thought again, today was the day. She hugged the secret to herself, delighting in it, anticipating how things would be a few hours later.

Her phone showed that there were two new messages, though no calls.

She looked at the messages. One was from the service provider, reminding her that she was low on currency. She would need to put in some more money if her prepaid connection was to remain active. She made a mental note. She had to keep it live, today of all days. Luckily, even fifty rupees would do, and she had that much to spare.

But the other was from him. Her face lit up, and her lips curved in a smile as she opened the message slowly and read what was written there. 'Aahi aasu' it said in Assamese, their language. 'I'm coming.'

They had devised, between them, a system of missed calls that 'spoke', without being charged. Quickly, she speed-dialled his number, and waited. One ring, two. She put it down, smiling. He would know she was awake. She turned down the volume of her phone, because she did not want to wake up her parents beyond the bamboo partition.

Promptly, the phone buzzed. One-two-three. 'I love you.' The smile on her face grew broader. It was just like in the movies, really. Better, because it was happening in real life. And it was happening to her.

Hugging the delicious secret to herself, she got down quietly from the bamboo platform. Her mind was already leaping ahead, planning, anticipating, smiling a little with the joy of what would happen in a few hours.

Outside, her mother was already at the hand pump, washing her face and getting ready for her day. She ran a small tea shack at the fork in the main highway. Deuta helped out sometimes, but after his illness, he was not really up to much. And so, once a fortnight, it was she, Maini, who went into the village, and bought the stuff needed to keep the tea shack going.

'Get ready soon, Maini', said her mother. 'That shop gets crowded fast. Come back before the traffic thickens and the customers start arriving.'

She had readied her clothes yesterday itself, and now, after her bath near the hand pump, she took them from the alna. She put on her red mekhela, the one she had woven herself. She arranged a red-bordered white sador around her body, finally pinning the aansol to her red blouse. Kajol on her eyes, a big red phot on her forehead, her hair plaited into a long beni that snaked down to below her hips. Suddenly, she felt a shyness overtake her. But she put her comb and a small mirror into the cloth bag that she carried.

In the kitchen, near the wood-fired souka, sat her father, drinking his tea out of a metal bowl. Maini looked at him. Ever since his illness, he had aged.

She kept her phone carefully beside her near the wooden pira as she sat down to have the pressed rice that was their breakfast.

'I'm going to the shops today, deuta', Maini said, affectionately. 'What shall I get you?'

Her father smiled. 'I have everything. But you take care. These roads, so many vehicles from the town now, and those bikes…'

'Don't worry, deuta, I'll be fine', she said.

She took up the phone again, and tucked it into the bag.

Her mother was outside, preparing to leave for the shop. She looked at Maini and said, 'White sador. It's a dusty road, you know.' But it was affectionately said. She was kind, her mother, but worn out now from all the hard work she needed to do.

'You remember what we need, don't you? And the money, you've taken it?'

Maini nodded, and moved out towards the bamboo gate.

Her mother watched her as she walked away with youthful, happy steps. Of course, she was in love, she thought. She was glad for this happiness that had come to her daughter. She only wished, now, that it would be a suitable boy, somebody like them, like her own husband, who would make a caring husband for her. She had heard Maini talk in whispers every night, after the household was supposed to be asleep, on the phone.

Maini walked down the narrow path carefully. The November sun was out, and everything around was glorious and golden, as though she was walking through a field of ripe paddy.

She felt the little pouch slung across her body. Yes, the phone was there. It was her life now, and she didn't know what she would do without it. It had changed her life in a wholly unexpected way, and would, she thought, be instrumental in changing it further. That thousand rupees, not a small sum, was worth every paisa.

Her mind wandered to how it had started.

It was a month after she had bought the phone, when the call came. It was not from a number that she recognised. Getting a call was still a novelty in itself.

She had just got into bed, after charging her phone at the one electrical socket in the house.

'Hello', she answered, timidly. She still felt strange saying this word. But she felt bold and daring, yes, even empowered, though she did not know the word itself. Saying hello into a phone she had bought with her own money made her feel like that girl, that journalist in that Hindi movie, who moved around on her own wearing jeans and a tee that showed the curves on her body, and did things that made the high and mighty tremble on their thrones.

'Hello', replied a voice she did not recognise. A male voice. 'Koney koisey? Who's speaking?'

'Maini', she answered. Too late, she remembered her friend Bhonita's instructions. 'Don't give your name to just anybody who asks for it on the phone. Ask who he or she is first, if you don't recognise the voice.' Bhonita had been a phone owner for over a year now, and Maini had listened to her tips on phone etiquette gratefully. After all, nobody had a phone in their house yet, not even deuta. Hers was the first.

'Maini... beautiful name.'

Maini stiffened. Was this a flirtation? One of those that began with a random call. If things went all right, it developed into a friendship. It was, she had heard, quite common. A timepass thing, a way to 'get to know each other'.

But almost immediately, she relaxed. Even if it was, how did it matter? He wouldn't know where she stayed; it was harmless. Several of the girls she knew had this 'special phone friend' with whom they discussed things and flirted after work. Sometimes they met, and one or two even got into a relationship with the person. It was fun, and there was no harm in seeing where this went. Now that she had a phone, this was part of all the good things that went with it, she supposed.

'Hoy ne?' she asked, coquettishly, softening her voice so that it was higher pitched, and more girlish. 'Is that so? And what's yours?' She used the familiar 'tumi' for him, instead of 'apuni', as would have befitted the situation, since she was addressing a stranger and a man.

'Premodhor', he answered. 'Premodhor Kalita.'

He sounded friendly, she thought. Premodhor... Prem. Love.

'Your name is nice, too', she said. She asked, 'Why did you call this number?'

'No, it was by mistake', he said. 'Wrong number', but he laughed. She knew exactly why he was laughing. He must be one of those who were looking for love, or at least a relationship, a telephonic one to begin with. Calls were cheap, and usually, these men and women made ten or twelve random calls a day. Most of the time, nothing materialised. But sometimes, often enough to keep the game going, something did.

Yes, it was a common enough thing. Along with the many freedoms that this little gadget had brought to them, had come this. The freedom to flirt, to have a telephonic conversation with a member of the opposite sex, in secret. It was a delicious thing, and even if nothing came of it, it was good to have a friend at the other end of this little gadget.

'Wrong number, I see', she said, still speaking in her telephone voice. 'So there's no need to continue this conversation, is there?'

'No, wait, what's the hurry?' he asked. 'Your voice is like the sound of a bird. Let me listen to it some more.'

'A bird. A crow?' They had both laughed. She liked the way he laughed, too. Open, without inhibitions. And then his voice was nice, too. She was judging him, she realised, by the sound of his voice alone, as he sounded on her phone. It was a cheap gadget, and surely must have changed the way his voice was transmitted to her. But still.

This was delightful. And because of the newness of this game, there were no rules or social restrictions yet that came down on her, an unmarried village girl, if she looked too long at a boy, or was seen speaking to a man not a relative. Oh, of course there would be disapproval if people were to find out. But the great thing about these phone flirtations was that nobody would know, nobody could really find out, could they, unless she chose to tell them herself. And it was so harmless, such a feel-good thing, it would be a pity to just say 'Sorry, wrong number' in a brisk voice and end the call.

And so it had started.

Next night, too, at about the same time, the call came. Even though the number flashed on the screen, Maini knew, without looking at it, that it was him. Premodhor. Prem. Should she call him that?

Timorously, amazed at her own daring, she received the call, and said, 'Premodhor?' Then, because it sounded too bold, she added, hastily, 'Dada?'

Calling him 'elder brother' softened the whole thing, somehow.

'Hello, Maini', he said, easily. He seemed not to have noticed her nervousness. But then how would he know, just by the sound of her voice, whether she was happy or sad, nervous or angry? 'Bhaal lagisey; it's good that you are calling me dada. But how do you know I am older than you? How old are you, anyway?'

She wasn't too sure about her age, but had a rough idea. About twenty. But something about the anonymity that this little red gadget afforded her, or perhaps some cautionary instinct, made her hesitate. 'I'm older than you think, you know', she said.

'In that case, I'll call you baideo, elder sister, if you are', he had responded promptly. But then he waited.

'I'm forty', she said. 'Twice twenty. And you?'

'I'm twenty. Once', he laughed.

She wanted to imbue this voice at the other end of the line with qualities that she wanted him to possess. And here they were, in actual fact, the same age.

'Premo, I'll call you that', she said, pleased that his name fit the concept that she had in mind.

'Maini. Such a lovely name. Is your phone a smartphone? Can you take pictures?'

'No, it's just a simple thing. I only got it recently.'

'Ah', he said. 'With a smartphone, we could have video calls with each other.' He paused, then added, 'I'm just a college boy; mine is not a smartphone, either.'

She preferred it this way, to have visual anonymity, so that even if they crossed each other on the road, they would not know it was them.

And, just like that, life changed for Maini. It became a routine for her, something she looked forward to at the end of the day. It was like a deadline she had because he called at ten. Every night. This was late in their parts. And it was almost always he who called because he had a talk plan that allowed him free local calls.

'I'm supposed to be studying', he said once. He stayed in the college hostel in the town, he had told her, but casually.

Mostly, though, they did not talk about their domestic arrangements. She had filled in details of her supposed life as a forty-year-old only sketchily, saying she lived with her parents because she had never married. He, too, hardly spoke about college life. They talked about things like a movie they had recently seen or a festival in progress. In this relationship, other details were not important, or even required. They were two disembodied voices, two people who were getting, increasingly, drawn to each other. When they spoke to each other, it was as they themselves, their identities shorn of the environment in which they lived. They were just themselves, without the trappings of family, job, occupation, or age. The way they looked, whether they were fat or thin, attractive or not… none of it mattered. It was the best she could be, during these conversations, without the imperatives of needing to be accepted, that were so strongly present in the real world around her. There were none of the boundaries that the village placed on her.

She found herself making mental notes throughout the day as she moved about her chores. 'I must tell Premo this', she would think, walking through the fields. When a leech latched on to her toe and blood seeped out, her first thought was, 'I wonder what Premo will say when I tell him about this.'

And he always did react, very empathetically.

They devised a system of missed calls, and throughout the day, as she went about her chores, she 'spoke' to him in their code. One short ring meant 'Thinking about you'. Three was, what else, 'I love you'. He too would reply in the same code. It brought a sparkle to her eyes and a warmth to her cheeks, when these calls that spoke their own private language came.

If their age difference bothered him, he didn't talk about it. And Maini hugged her secret to herself, waiting for the day when she could tell him that they were the same age, in reality. They had accepted each other as friends, or indeed, as something more than friends, and their respective ages did not matter. Not all relationships could be pinned down with names. This was one of them. Technology had brought them together, and language still hadn't invented a label for the relationship that they had.

And one day, just like that, as they were talking, he had said, 'I think we should meet.' He sounded diffident, but said again, more firmly, 'Yes, we should meet.'

Her heart sang, but just in time, she remembered. 'All right. But why would you want to meet me? A forty-year-old woman?'

He paused. When he replied, it was with the air of somebody who had thought about it. Slowly, he said, 'Well. You know, there is this thing. Older woman, younger man. Younger boy, you can say.'

'How can that be', she said. 'I have always only heard of the opposite. Younger woman, older man.'

'Priyanka Chopra?' he reminded her.

'Oh yes', she remembered. Well, if that was how he looked at their relationship, she had no problems. She hoped, though, that when they finally met, and they turned out to be the same age, he would not have any difficulties adjusting to the reality.

She made up her mind.

'Yes. Let's meet.'

And so, here she was, dressed carefully, walking through dusty paths in order to meet him, carrying a bright yellow cloth bag.

'How will I recognise you, then?' she had asked, after dates and times and places had been discussed.

'I'll be on a cycle. It's black.'

'Our village has as many black cycles as there are white cows', she had laughed.

'Well...' he had fallen silent.

She remembered that she would not look like the kind of person he would be expecting. 'All right', she had said. 'We'll carry something... a mona, a cloth bag? I have a yellow one, woven. I'll carry that.'

'All right', he had said, but doubtfully. 'I have a black one, woven also.'

'Black cycle, black bag...' she had laughed, 'Everything you possess is black?'

He had laughed, too. 'No, I'll wear white. A white panjabi and dhuti.'

She had been surprised. Twenty-year-old boys in their village hardly ever wore the draped dhuti. 'You wear a dhuti?' she had asked, surprised.

'Not all the time', he had answered. 'But this will be a special occasion.'

'Okay, I'll wear my white sador. I only wear it for very special occasions. But then this is one. You'll recognise me that way. Nobody wears a white sador to the shops on workdays; everything is too dusty.'

'And of course we'll have our phones. We'll call each other, won't we, when we reach the crossroads you mentioned?' he had asked.

She took out the phone once more now as she walked along. Past the familiar fields, through paths she had crossed over and again, ever since she could walk. He wouldn't look at her at first, of course. He would be expecting a woman twice her age. But she hoped his eyes would stop at her, linger for a while before moving on. She knew she looked good today.

She was almost at the crossroads. The path was now wider, a road, almost, and there were many people around.

Her phone rang.

Heart beating, she took it out. Yes, it was him.

'I'm here, in front of the shop, where are you?'

'I'm here too', she answered, looking around.

'I don't see... wait.' He rang off. Still holding her phone, she looked around.

There were many people here, at the crossroads near the provision shop. Men, women of all ages, several on bicycles. Black. She looked at them. Two women in mekhela sadors were cycling, probably to the main market. A middle-aged man with grey hair. A young man, wearing glasses, looking towards her. She gazed at him, enraptured. But no. The young man looked away and cycled on. Besides, he was wearing dark trousers. Not a dhuti.

She turned around. No, there was nobody behind her. She brought her phone forward, and was about to call him, when it rang.

'I can't see you Maini', he said. 'Where are you?'

She looked around, and ahead. The man with grey hair, wearing a white dhuti, with a black bag slung on his shoulder, was standing beside a black cycle, and speaking into a small phone.

She didn't answer immediately.

'Hello. Maini?'

She could see his lips move, the man's, as though he was lip synching in some stage play.

She weighed her options, even as his voice grew more urgent. She could switch off her phone, turn around and never answer his number again. Or…

Slowly, with a small smile, she moved forward. 'Look ahead', she said. 'I have a surprise for you too.'

My People in Paradise

Bashabi Fraser

I was born on a lake. You may not believe me, but this is true. This is no fairy tale, though you may think I am talking about a make-believe world. I was born on a boat, not because my mother was going anywhere, but because we lived on a boat and that was not very long ago, till everything changed. Our boat was one of many, moored along the side of a vast lake that reflected the heavens, so the mood of the sky decided the mood of the water, bursting with laughter when the sun sparkled in splendour, heavy with worries when dark clouds rolled over the mountains and surrounded us with gloom, but dancing with abandon when the rains came to cheer up the water which felt renewed and young again.

We were the boat people, living in floating houses, and we could visit each other in smaller boats, and some were so close, we could jump across from one to the next. We did jump on to the shore to walk to school, feeling the solid ground underneath, which did not feel quite real. I have walked with my father to the shops in the city. I have ridden on the handlebar of my father's bicycle to collect the warm cloth from weavers' houses in villages just outside the city. He packed the cloth in a big, tall bundle and piled it high on the back seat. I helped him to tie it tightly with ropes, and the ride back to our lake colony was slower than the ride out. I have even ridden cycle vans with my grandfather before he died peacefully in his bed. He used to hire a van to carry the shawls, tunics and hats my mother, grandmother, father, my uncles, aunties and cousins embroidered with patterns that told stories of this heaven on earth, of our flowers and leaves, our rivers, lakes and trees in colours that are certainly made in heaven. In fact, my grandfather used to say that where we lived was heaven on earth. I believed him, for what could be more beautiful than the country around our boat people? And the lake was our mother. I can't say motherland, for it was anything but solid. But it rocked us to sleep and lapped around our dreams and desires. It gave us the certainty and love that a mother gives us, always there, emotionally charged but true.

My older brother was twelve years older than I was. My mother had named him Rayan, as he grew luxuriantly like the reeds watered by our lake, at heaven's gate. My father was quite sad when my brother decided against going to university to study law as my father had always dreamed he would, for after my brother finished school he took over the wanderer's business from our father. He said he wanted to see the world, but I think he was like a tethered Arab steed. He wanted to get away. He had a glint in his blue eyes that looked for adventure.

Just before the snow came, he slung a big bundle over his shoulder which I could not lift when I tried. He laughed and said, one day I would be able to lift it and we could have two such bundles and go away together. Where did he go? He said he took the train to faraway cities and he visited some families every year who had become like family to him. They looked out for him and waited for him every winter. The women were particularly kind to him. He spread out a shawl on the carpets and mats or cold marble or cement floors and displayed the shawls and tunics which fluttered before his spellbound hostesses like so many birds from heaven. He didn't take the hats, as the city folk were not too keen on them. But the shawls were the most popular. They rippled and shimmered over the arms and shoulders of the grandmothers, mothers, wives and daughters, like the waves of our lake. He spoke with particular fondness of two women, Deepa bhabhi in Ahmedabad and Shefali boudi in Kolkata. He never ate any food in any of the houses he visited, but he could not refuse Deepa bhabhi's sherbet and Shefali boudi's coffee. They had his drink brought to him by their cook soon after he arrived at their door.

Rayan felt locked in by the mountains surrounding our lake and he wanted to see the whole wide world. He wanted to plant his feet on ground that didn't move and he wanted to sleep in rooms which were not swayed by the restless waves of a lake that seemed forever awake. He did tell me that he preferred the rocking of the trains that ambled over several rivers and wound across widening plains, a rhythm he said was more constant and predictable than the urgency or complacency of our lake waters, ruled by the hues of the heavens above. He said the trains took him away from the same dawns, promising nothing different as each day stretched on without promise of change.

He had only one regret.

He had seen Reema one day in the market, her scarf blown back by a wind that brought change in his life and ours. Her green eyes brought the breath of the forests she came from and was named after, as they looked for salvation from his sky-reflecting glance. But we were lake folk and they were people who trusted the trees that had protected them for centuries. How could trees now walk to the waters' edge and feel safe there? Our families felt the two could only marry and live together in another world. However, no one could stop them from meeting. When Rayan took visitors who wanted a spin round the lake, Reema became his co-oarsman. She accompanied him, sitting with her legs swinging from a cycle van, when he insisted on giving my father a rest from collecting the woven warm fabric from the village near the forest where the forest meditated on a babbling river that flowed below the gentle slopes. My brother was as gentle as the undulating lush land where Reema met him and they sat on the edge of the mountain stream letting the same waves kiss one pair of feet, then another, in a healing ritual that felt like a divine blessing.

But he was wrong—this handsome brother of mine, whose hair looked like burnished gold with a crimson tinge when the sun played with it. *This* was paradise, his paradise where Reema was and she was not far away—just across the stream, waiting where the pine trees stood stolid and protective. And I, his princess, his little Sofia, knew this to be the truth. But Rayan was restless. He had no time to study law. What would he do with a law degree when communities decided what was theirs by right and sliced up the world into compartments of those who were always right and decided others were always wrong—as they had done for so many years? They believed the lake people were different from the city people, who were different from the forest people, who were different from the valley people, who were different from the plains and city people. Yet we were all the same, weren't we? We all had our families to love and be nurtured by, we lived and needed the comfort and security of our homes, we looked forward to our meals with our families, we were reliant on the sun, clouds and rains, and wove and embroidered our lives in ways we knew, making them appealing and meaningful and sustaining. Why did we think we were all so different? It was a question I took many years to fathom and answer for myself.

Soon my unruly hair was gathered into a neat long plait. Rayan could no longer ruffle my hair when he came back once the snow had melted as I was almost as tall as he was and I could move away swiftly whenever I saw his mischievous hand reaching out to pull my plait.

And he could never wait to see his forest girl. But Reema was not ready to sit by the stream or be his co-oarsman anymore. She was finding it difficult to stop her family from finding her a suitable groom. How long could she wait? Rayan found it difficult to appease her. All his honey words only annoyed her. She warned him, 'One more winter, and I'll be someone else's bride.' Rayan knew this was her ultimatum to him. Yes, he now had big plans for their future. He would start a business that would take the shawls and tunics and even the hats to faraway lands, where it was always cold and the people there would need them. He asked our family to make embroidered coats as well for his future clients. How would he organise this? He would send them on planes to a distant city. Deepa bhabhi had a cousin in Leicester, Amar, who had a shop which would sell Rayan's goods, and Shefali boudi's husband, who worked for the airlines, could arrange for the cargo to be flown to England from the airport in their very own lake city. So people from far and near, people who had not met us and only knew Rayan, were ready to help him. It meant that our vibrant colours and magical designs on warm fabrics would wrap around those people who would feel the touch of love and comfort woven into the garments. That year my family, and other lake folk worked extra hard to make the goods ready for Rayan's planned journey. The tourists who used to come to take a boat ride had thinned out, so there was more time to sit in our boat homes and sew and stitch as the boats trembled gently, anchored along the shoreline.

The order was paid for in advance by Amar in Leicester, and the cargo was lifted onto the plane which we watched becoming a speck in the cloudless sky till it faded across the horizon which Rayan looked at longingly. But now he had the money to marry Reema, and her family was relieved to see her settle down as she was considered too old by the eligible men of their village and their neighbouring villages. And my mother could buy new carpets to replace the threadbare ones and the boat people could buy more coal for their braziers. Life felt good.

I could now fulfil my father's dream and study law, and I borrowed my father's bicycle to go to the college where I was one of five women students and the rest were men, who eyed us eagerly, driving us into a cluster of protective femininity. We went to the cafeteria together and ordered samosas which my mother never made in our boathouse. And for the first time I tasted the coffee Rayan had spoken about that Shefali boudi used to make for him in Kolkata. It felt like forbidden fruit from the east of Eden, aromatic and energising. I suddenly felt grown up and emboldened. I was no longer the twelve years younger sister, my father's little princess, but a woman who felt a free wind on her back. However, our lecturers seemed on edge, sensing a changing wind, a storm gathering somewhere else. The water of our lake grew murky and the sky above us glowered with a hidden unvented anger. As I rode to the law college, I noticed more boots marching than rambling shoes and ambling sandals.

There was one lecturer whose classes we really looked forward to. She taught human rights and looked directly at our group of five when she spoke of women's rights. She had examples of cases on her fingertips. When hands shot up with challenging questions from some of the young men, her gaze did not falter and she told us it was important not just to know what the law was but where it was, which volume, which page number. She told us we needed to keep on top of verdicts being passed elsewhere, which we could cite as precedents. We called her Professor Sarkar, and she moved with the authority and confidence her knowledge gave her.

One day she surprised us by walking to our table in the cafeteria and said she was going to order another round of coffee and samosas for all of us. Never had a teacher joined us like this. She had something to tell us. That was when we learned about Amnesty International, a worldwide body which campaigned for people they did not necessarily know but whose human dignity, safety, well-being and freedom were their concern. We were amazed. These people were like Deepa bhabhi and Shefali boudi who helped people in distant lands, from whom they did not wish to gain anything. She asked us if we would like to support Amnesty for that was what justice was about, defending the fundamental rights of all human beings. We were mesmerised by her courage and audacity.

But the next day, Professor Sarkar did not come for her lecture. We waited for half an hour, and when we walked into the corridor, we overheard the boys saying they had heard from a classmate who had seen her with two packed suitcases taking a taxi and directing it to the railway station. We didn't need to discuss our next step. One of the girls always had a car at her disposal as her father wanted her watched and escorted at all times. We all piled into the immaculate Hyundai which tore through the heavily patrolled streets and spilled us out near the platform minutes before the guard blew the whistle. We spotted Professor Sarkar at a window at the same moment as she looked at us, surprised, and waved. We were breathless. I could only ask, 'Why?' She knew what I meant. 'I believe that a university classroom is for interchange, questions and debate. I can't do that while facing the barrel of a gun.' After a brief pause, she added, 'I won't forget you. Remember, my name is Shanti. Call me Shanti di if you will, but not Professor Sarkar. I will be in London. I have work to do there.' We could only nod and hold back our tears. There were too many boots and barrels at the station, keeping watch. We had to stay calm.

That night Reema who was staying at her parents' house, felt her waters break. Rayan and his father-in-law asked a neighbour to drive her in their three-wheeler mini truck to the hospital in the city. But where were the lights of the city? It seemed as if the city had disappeared overnight. They were barricaded at a checkpoint which had appeared like a fierce genie. Rayan and his father-in-law were dragged out. Their neighbour who was driving fled into the darkness while shots broke the silence of the forest behind. When the neighbours found Reema as dawn broke, she was sprawled on the car seat, but still breathing and on the floor of the truck next to the gearbox, was a tiny boy with blue eyes, bloody and kicking, screaming for attention.

My father and my cousins did not come back one evening when they had gone to the city to buy food and meet retailers for the warm cloths the boat people looked forward to embellishing with their dreams and designs. We waited through brooding dark days for them. The phones had died. Was there still another world out there? But amidst all this, like a pigeon carrying a message from another world, came a plane ticket with papers from Shefali boudi, sent through a grim messenger which asked me to join Professor Sarkar's—no, Shanti di's—course in London. My mother said it was best to leave as we had no home left. Maybe I could help to find my father, Rayan, Reema's father and my cousins with the help of good people there who didn't know us but were concerned about us. Our lake had been sold as had been the forest behind Reema's village. It was all for our benefit. Our heaven on earth remained, but the people I knew who lived there had melted like the spring snow without a trace. Yet I know they were once there, that they breathed the air in paradise which was their home.

Masquerades and Masks

A Little Light Reading

Yasmine Gooneratne

My husband's specialist area of research relates to the cultures of Asia. He explored this area very successfully in his teaching after his appointment to the staff of an Australian university in New South Wales, and he made a documentary on Sri Lanka too, which has helped to make his name known and respected worldwide. That name, which was originally Bharat (meaning 'India'), he changed to Barry (a name very familiar to most Australians) after he realised that an English name would be more acceptable to our fellow-Australians than an 'exotic' oriental one that they found difficult to spell or pronounce.

We've all seen my husband's documentary film about Sri Lanka so often on international TV that there's no point describing it here. When it was shown for the first time on Australian national television, it was such a success that his university came in for a good deal of favourable publicity. Maybe I'm biased, but I thought the best thing about the film was Barry himself. He came over as charming and witty. As well, of course, as extremely handsome. For now that he had shed his spectacles and was into contact lenses, Barry proved remarkably photogenic. So much so that in various TV interviews he gave afterwards, it didn't really seem to matter what he said because he looked so terrific saying it. And I'm not the only person who thought so. Barry received bags of mail from people who had seen him on TV, and most of the letters were from women.

In my husband's fan mail one day there was a letter from a jewellery designer who had recorded an interview he had given

---

Editors' note: This story, adapted from Chapter 24 of Gooneratne's novel *A Change of Skies*, is narrated by a young married woman of Sri Lankan (Tamil) origin, who has accompanied her Sinhalese husband to Australia.

on 'The Midday Show'. She had stopped the film, she wrote, at a particular point to have a closer look at a jewelled earring from the Sigiriya rock fortress, which Barry had held up to the camera. This piece had fascinated her. But then she had looked past the earring, as it were, to the palm on which it was displayed. She had been able to pause the frame long enough to get a good look at Barry's palm and the lines on it.

She then wrote to him:

'Have you ever had your palm read, Professor Mundy? The path your lifeline takes indicates to me that profound changes are occurring in your life. If you are to make the most of your potential, you must be prepared to shed the past and begin anew.'

With her letter she sent Barry a little package of booklets she had published on the subjects of astrology, palmistry and the occult sciences. She had read his palm, she said, and charted a horoscope for him, and in that she had found a clear prediction that he would marry a woman of a nationality different from his own.

She added her telephone number.

Now, although ours is what they call at home in Sri Lanka an 'arranged marriage', because both sets of parents have given it their support and encouragement, it is also a love marriage. We met and fell in love. I am quite, quite sure that nobody else could possibly take my place in Barry's affections. There's no question about it, our relationship is a very special one, based on love, trust and mutual respect—although it is also a traditional marriage of the old-fashioned kind.

But despite that, I have always avoided reminding Barry about that prediction in his horoscope that he would marry a woman of a different nationality.

Especially after we came to Australia.

I wondered now whether this jewellery designer was an attractive woman; and if so, whether the powers that be might find their effectiveness reduced by our emigration to another country. I couldn't get it out of my head that in Australia there are something like eight million women of 'another nationality', all of them, probably, devotees of 'The Midday Show'.

While waiting in the check-out queue in our local supermarket, I began with increasing misgivings to study the predictions for Barry's week and mine in the 'You and Your Stars' pages of *New Idea* and *The Women's Weekly*. Whenever they predicted romance for him, or advised caution for one or either of us, I worried myself sick about it for the rest of the week.

I thought of writing to amma, and asking her advice, but thought better of it. 'You're becoming neurotic, Jean', I told myself firmly one day. 'Stop it. This won't do.'

And it was just at that very moment that the telephone rang. It was Francesca Sweetlips, asking me whether she could bring the jewellery designer to tea with me one afternoon.

Dr Sweetlips has always been a great help to Barry in his research, and of course I said yes. Especially since, according to her, the visit might greatly aid Barry's research into Asian culture, the jewellery designer being in a position to contribute a great deal to it due to her exhaustive knowledge of the occult sciences of Asia.

'Be unto your husband as Sita, as Sakuntala, as Savitri', the old brahmin from our family kovil had instructed me on our wedding day, invoking those heroic models of female duty, devotion and resourcefulness that amma has always advised me to adopt as my own in my married life.

So I decided to do my very best on Barry's behalf, and when the day of our little tea party arrived, I made samosas, a chocolate cake, and a pumpkin pie from an American recipe that Barry's sister Veera had sent me from New York. Altogether, it was quite an occasion, especially since with all this delicious food I also served some High Country Special, the tea that comes from my brother-in-law Asoka's estate.

The jewellery designer arrived, wearing some of her own creations in her ears and on both arms, as well as on her ankles and toes. She told Francesca and me over tea that palmistry was only one of her many interests. Asia fascinated her, she said, with all its mysteries, its eroticism, its religious symbolism and its ancient cults. She knew a great deal about both astrology and numerology, and was herself born under the sign of Capricorn.

'Amma would love to meet you', I told her. And it was true, because my mother is a great believer in the stars, and in horoscopes, and even in folk superstition. She has lived in cities almost all her life, but will never set out on a journey, or even step out of doors if a gecko on the wall has tchk-tchked its danger signal. And if she ever loses something valuable, her keys for instance, or a legal document, or a piece of jewellery, she always consults the light reader.

'What's a light reader, Jean?' Francesca asked.

'I think you'd call her a clairvoyant here', I said. 'Amma's favourite light reader lives in a tiny house in the Pettah in Colombo. Her family, all of them fortune-tellers and light readers, have lived in that quarter for generations. She can usually "find" what you've lost without so much as moving from her seat in front of her lighted candle, but occasionally, in more difficult cases, she will come and stay a few days in your house until she receives the right vibrations. According to amma, she hasn't had a failure yet.'

The designer was most interested to hear about my mother, whom she said she instantly recognised as a kindred spirit.

'Do you take after your mother, Mrs Mundy?' she asked me.

'Oh, I hope so', I replied. 'In some things, at any rate. Which reminds me—do you mind telling me just what you had in mind when you wrote to my husband that he must prepare to shed the past and begin anew?'

The designer looked a bit uncomfortable. I was standing close beside her, and when I spoke, I had a very long, highly polished silver knife in my hand, with which I happened to be cutting the chocolate cake. And then again, she is not a tall person like Francesca, and she was perched on a high stool at the breakfast counter in our kitchen while we talked. Maybe it was too high for her.

'The lines on your husband's palm were not clear enough to be exact about that', she said. 'It could be his field of study. Perhaps your husband will branch out in new directions, into fresh areas of intellectual exploration, a complete change of life.'

'Well, that's a relief', I said. 'For a while I wondered if the fates had decreed a change of wife.'

This seemed to strike the designer as an extremely witty and amusing remark, for she laughed quite loudly at it, as did Francesca, and that certainly surprised me, for I don't think Francesca sees me generally as a particularly clever or witty person. The whole occasion went very well, especially when we began to talk of Asian food, for the designer (who said she was taking a course in advanced Chinese cooking) became so interested in the subject that I took my collection of cookery books off the kitchen bookshelf, and all three of us discussed and exchanged recipes.

When the designer left, Francesca stayed on. And after a while she returned to the subject of the occult.

'Jean', she said, 'What would you do if you lost something valuable?'

'If I were in Sri Lanka, I'd go and see amma's light reader right away', I said.

'But if you lost it here, in Australia?'

'That would be what the light reader calls a "difficult case", since it would involve transmitting her powers over a considerable distance. But her methods would work perfectly well, just the same.'

I told Francesca about the time my mother had discovered, during appa's spell as Sri Lanka's high commissioner in London, that her diamond brooch was missing. There had been a spate of cat burglaries in British cities just then, and amma thought a window at the high commission hadn't been properly closed, so that the thief had been able to climb in that way. She didn't bother calling Scotland Yard: instead, she just cabled Colombo. The light reader was immediately consulted, and her findings were cabled back to amma in London:

> I see your precious jewel lie
> Fallen, beneath an alien sky.
> Search for it without delay
> In the Four-Wheeled Chariot's way.

'Goodness', Francesca said. 'Whatever did that mean?'

'As soon as she read the cable', I said, 'Amma remembered that the evening before the loss of the brooch was discovered, she and appa had attended a reception at the French embassy. She rang His Excellency right away, and then sent appa's secretary post-haste over there. He came back with the diamond brooch, which he'd found lying just where she had dropped it in the embassy driveway as she got into the car after the reception.'

'Wow, that was really a bit of luck!' Francesca said, then paused before continuing. 'And, Jean, if something valuable isn't just lost, but… taken away?'

'Oh, do you mean "stolen"?' I said. 'Well, that calls for special methods, I believe. Rather like the way down in Matara—that's south of Colombo—they call in devil dancers to exorcise the evil spirits when a spell has been placed on a person by some ill-wisher.'

'Like the blessing of a house by a clergyman to dispel ghosts that might be haunting it after someone has died?'

'Not quite', I replied. 'Because a theft, like a spell, involves using a counter-spell to defeat it. Or a charm. Or poison.'

'A-a charm? P-poison?'

Francesca shivered a little. She comes from an American community that had, she told me once, burned quite a number of witches in the seventeenth century, and I suppose she associated what I was saying with witchcraft and bubbling cauldrons. On the other hand, the sun had just gone down, and the air had a slight chill to it. So, I put the kettle on, made another pot of High Country Special, and poured two cups for Francesca and myself.

'Yes, poison', I said, passing her the milk. 'You see, once the stolen article has been located and the thief identified, the loser has a choice. One can simply go along, confront the thief and retrieve the article. But, if one's feeling revengeful, one can ask the light reader to punish the thief by casting a spell on him. Or her.'

'What sort of a spell?' Francesca asked.

'Oh, the spells vary', I said. 'As far as I know, amma has never had to resort to doing that sort of thing. Nor would she wish to. But other people aren't as forgiving and generous-minded as my mother. One of my aunts, they say, who is terribly bad-tempered, had such a vicious spell cast upon a man who had stolen coconuts from her estate that he broke out in the most awful boils and sores. The sores covered his whole body, and they stank like anything. Nothing could cure him.'

Francesca said nothing. She had stopped sipping her tea.

'And then there's the story they tell in Barry's family about an ancestress of his who was preparing to elope with a manservant. They had delayed in arranging a marriage for her, you see, and the poor thing had fallen in love with her brother's valet. Well, their plan was discovered, and the family, aware that she had a headstrong nature, realised that desperate measures were called for. So they called in the family charmist, and a spell was secretly prepared to end the love affair.'

'What happened to her?' Francesca asked.

'To him. The girl crept quietly down the stairs on the appointed night, and climbed into the carriage, where her lover sat waiting for her, just as they had planned. Except that his head was missing.'

'Oh, my god.'

'It happened a very long time ago, Francesca', I said reassuringly. 'In the eighteenth century, I think. And it all ended happily. The family arranged the girl's marriage soon afterwards, and she ended up a plump, comfortable matron, mother of a family of four children. That sort of thing wouldn't happen nowadays, of course. At least, I don't think so. Though it still features on the light reader's tariff.'

'T-tariff?'

'Of Special Services Available on Demand. That's shorthand, of course, for "Very Expensive". Much more expensive, for instance, than getting amma's diamond brooch back, which was quite a simple operation. The choice really depends on how valuable the lost article is to the person who lost it. But whether a case is simple or difficult, my mother is absolutely convinced—the method never fails.'

Francesca pushed her cup away from her.

'I really must go, Jean', she said. 'Essays to correct.'

She had left her handbag in our bathroom, she said, and she went to get it. When she came back she was paler than ever, almost as if she had been sick. I felt concerned.

'Francesca, are you sure you wouldn't like to rest for a while before you go? Barry could easily drive you home when he gets back.'

'No, oh no, Jean, I'm quite all right.' She was very quick about putting on her coat and scarf. 'It must have been a relief for your mother, to get her brooch back', she said, a trifle shakily. 'What an extraordinary thing, that no one at the French embassy had found it.'

I smiled as I remembered amma's comment: 'It doesn't say much for the efficiency of Madame Henriet's gardeners, does it!' Being the soul of tact, she didn't say that in her letter of thanks to the French ambassador.

'She was very glad to have it back', I told Francesca. 'It wasn't just a valuable piece of jewellery, you see. She could have replaced that any time at Cartier's or Tiffany's when appa took up his next posting, which was to be in Washington. The brooch had sentimental value—my father gave it to her when they became engaged. I really believe she would have paid any amount, and done anything, to have it back.'

'Anything?'

'Oh, yes.'

'And she got it back quite undamaged?'

'Oh, absolutely', I said. 'Those Jaffna jewellers really know their craft. The American ambassador's big black Cadillac had rolled over it and bent the clasp a tiny bit, she told me, but otherwise it was as good as new, and she's worn it happily ever since.'

Francesca drove away, speeding rather dangerously at the corner, I thought. I was putting the tea things away when Barry got back from the university.

'Well, Jean, and what have you been up to all day?' he asked.

I told him all about the jewellery designer's visit, about my little tea party, and about the interesting conversation we'd had about clairvoyants and cooking.

'A typical housewife's afternoon, I see', was Barry's comment.

'Not quite. I've been doing some research, too', I said. I pointed to the kitchen counter, which still carried quite a load of cookery books, and also the booklets the jewellery designer had sent him.

'Oh?' said Barry politely. 'Nothing too taxing, I hope?'

'Just a little light reading', I said.

Talking Beasts

Rashida Murphy

'It's free', she said. 'A free service. Meaning you don't have to pay anything.' Sylvie sounded as tired as he felt. He knew he must smell bad too; her nose had twitched fractionally when she reached out to draw him into a hug. As usual, he hung back, stiff-armed and straight-spined while she tried to embrace him. There was way too much inter-sex hugging and cheek kissing in this country. At least, where he came from, men hugged men and women kissed women. His mother and sister kissed him on his forehead when he did something nice for them. That was how it was.

Sylvie looked around for somewhere to sit. He pushed at clothes and boxes on the mattress and gestured to the space he had created. She sat and he stood before her, not meeting her eyes, trying not to look at the white expanse of chest beneath the tank top. She was so tall that when they faced each other, his eyes were always at breast height with her. He shifted about, looking at his feet, wondering if he should sit next to her or spare her the odorous discomfort. He wished she had come a little later, wished she'd rung before arriving. He could have showered and changed. But he couldn't tell her that.

'The people are kind. I used to volunteer there when I was a student. Everyone works gratis, you know. Everyone. The lawyers, social workers, interpreters, everyone. I mean there's no charge for the services. And you could really use an interpreter. I know you understand English perfectly well but if they think…' Sylvie's voice faltered, and she didn't finish her sentence. She used lots of hand gestures when she spoke to him, something he thought she felt she had to do. She also repeated herself a lot. Short sentences. Repetition. She was a teacher after all. Old habits.

Aslam clicked his tongue at the word *lawyer*. A lawyer had caused the current mess he was in, anyway. Shirin had gone to a lawyer, suggested to her by that woman, Janet, who hated him.

Shirin told Aslam it was about convenience, and how it was no longer *convenient* for her to be with him. But Aslam heard her on the phone to her father, saying 'of course, abba' and 'yes, I'll tell him, abba'. Afterwards she told him her father had offered to pay her college fees for two years and instructed her to stop *fraternising* with Pakistani boys because she was being talked about.

'I do love you Aslam, and we can make it work.' Shirin held his hand and her ringed hand indicated the shabby room in the house they shared with two other (officially on the lease) couples.

Aslam stared at her and she continued, 'Abba will be really upset if he thinks we're still together. He'll make me go back. You know that. There are so many wagging tongues here, among our people. If he finds out I'm sharing a room with you... God, I don't even want to think what will happen. I'll move out temporarily, and abba will see how well I'm doing, and he won't care if I see you again. He thinks you're holding me back. I'm sorry. But for the next few months at least, we shouldn't see each other.'

Aslam told her he'd take on a couple of extra night shifts to pay for her new course, that fancy *Associate Degree in Criminology and Justice*, because the Cert IV in Hospitality was not good enough, even though they had both signed up for it as the easiest option. They had promised each other they would leave Australia together if they needed to—if studying and working their way into permanent residency didn't happen.

Shirin looked at him as if he had at last gone mad. 'You think your fifty bucks extra a week are going to pay for my course? Really Aslam. Why do you have to make everything so difficult?'

She flipped her hair back and gathered it in a loose knot at the nape of her neck and he thought he would die if he didn't see her every day. He saw how they all gathered around her, Pakistanis, Afghanis, Indians. The white boys loved her too. She wasn't shy, like other Asian girls. She gravitated into the centre of the crowd and they made room for her.

When they were children, it had been the other way around. Aslam was gregarious and popular, and Shirin the awkward, gangly one. Aslam the clown, the bringer of special treats, the instigator of forbidden escapades. Shirin hanging back, dependent on him.

And Aslam's mother, so kind, so loving to the only child of her dead best friend, reminding Aslam of his duty to look after the girl. Telling him to be careful when they played in the shadow of the great mosque, urging him to hold Shirin's hand in the storytellers' lane to protect her from the ghosts. What would ammi say if she could see him now, unable to hold on to the girl he had loved since he was five years old?

They'd met Janet at one of those compulsory lectures all overseas students had to attend, and the woman had become a permanent fixture in their lives since. Whispering, laughing, advising. Shirin started dressing differently, ditching her bangles and anklets and long hair and loose dresses for tight jeans and sleeveless tops. It made the boys look at her even more. Aslam wished Janet would have an accident one day. Drop dead. He'd cheer her demise and knew she wished him dead too, but Shirin laughed at them both and said they'd better get along, her favourite people. Then Janet brought in the lawyer. Not-yet-lawyer, Aslam reminded Shirin, and she flicked his cheek and told him not to be such a baby. The fellow was still studying but behaved like he knew everything. Words like *457 visas*, *sponsorships* and *in-demand courses* drifted around the house when the three of them talked, barely looking at Aslam as he clattered around, deliberately making his presence known. They talked about him as if he wasn't there. Janet once said, 'You don't want to end up like Aslam, do you?' when he walked in, dusty and hot after collecting trolleys all afternoon. Shirin turned to stare at him as if seeing him properly for the first time and he wanted to hit her then.

When he came home at six o'clock one Saturday evening, a week after that look, he knew something had shifted. Janet was in the kitchen, holding a mug of tea that she raised in the air when he walked in. He could hear voices and laughter in the front room. He stood still, staring at Janet till she put down her mug and brushed past him. Shirin turned as he entered, talking to that idiot lawyer who was wearing a blue suit today. He looked like a gigolo.

Shirin indicated the packed bags at her feet. 'I've found somewhere nice', she said cheerfully. 'Actually, Jake found it for me. You remember Jake. He's just finished the course I'm doing, so he's a real lawyer now.'

'You're leaving?' Aslam felt the sweat under the three-day-old shirt and folded his hands across his belly where the imprint of greasy trolleys was stamped. He licked his lips before he spoke, muscles aching with dehydration and hunger.

Janet brushed past him again and returned with a cup of tea. He took it and downed it in one gulp, thankful that Australians usually made their tea lukewarm and excessively milky.

'Just moving out temporarily, honey.' Shirin's voice was someone else's. She'd never called him *honey* before. Always *jaanum* or *mera budhoo*.

The gigolo-lawyer had already taken her bags to the waiting car and Janet stood between them, determined to prevent any scenes.

Aslam sat down on the rocking chair still covered with one of Shirin's old dupattas and took his shoes off. 'Go', he said. 'You'll never see me again. Be sure to tell my ammi this is your decision.'

'Are you threatening me? Don't be such an ass.' Shirin waved and walked out.

The car pulled away from the kerb with scarcely a sound and when Aslam looked up again, he was alone. He licked the last of the tea from the mug he still held and wondered if the others would notice if he ate some of the leftovers in the fridge. There was a strict rule that you did not eat what you hadn't made. All of them, Pakistanis and Indians alike, were uncomfortable with the rule because it went against the hospitality they were raised with. But they accepted it as fair because they worked odd hours and cooked when they could. To eat the food that someone was looking forward to after a long shift was wrong. Aslam did it anyway and threw the container in the council bin at the park. The Gujarati boy, whose dal and rice he had stolen, looked inside the fridge several times before he went out to buy a burger and chips.

Vegetarians were funny like that. They didn't mind eating meat if someone else cooked it for them.

When Aslam didn't turn up for work the next day, they fired him. His housemates were sympathetic but impatient. They all struggled with the courses they'd enrolled in to get their student visas, and the long hours they worked at supermarkets and petrol stations took the shine off their compassion.

'Talk to Sylvie, yaar', the Punjabi boy said to him, a week after Shirin's departure. 'She works with refugees and all. She's always offering help.'

'I'm not a refugee.' Aslam shouted.

The boy laughed. 'That's the spirit. She knows people and she can help. She wants to, doesn't she? Nice woman. Dresses nicely too.' The boy cupped his man boobs and slid his tee shirt off one shoulder.

'You have no shame.' Aslam walked outside to light a cigarette and the boy followed, giggling and remonstrating.

A few days later, Sylvie arrived. Tall, long-legged, compassionate Sylvie, who had once trekked through the Swat Valley and loved Kabul and Peshawar and imagined that's where *his people* came from. Trying to persuade him to go with her and ask for help—free help, she kept emphasising that—she looked ready to give up.

'Okay', Aslam said. 'I'll go. What should I say?'

'Tell them the truth. Ask for help. Mention what would happen if you went back. They know about the situation with the Hazaras. Tell them you are seeking asylum. And ask for an interpreter. Someone who speaks Dari.'

'I don't speak Dari. A little bit of Pashto, but mostly Punjabi and Urdu.'

'Of course, my mistake. So sorry. I always get the languages mixed up. Ah, it is stunning—that part of the world you come from, isn't it? The rivers, the tomato fields, that landscape. I wish I could go there again. Geez. I'm rambling. Sorry. I'm not doing you any favours by reminding you what you stand to lose. Urdu and Punjabi interpreters will be easier to find, so make sure you request one. I'll go with you the first time, but they will want to speak to you alone.'

The interpreter was a middle-aged Indian woman who reminded him of a kindly aunt. When the lawyer went out to get some tea, they chatted briefly about how nice it would be to get real chai with elaichi and adrak instead of the watery concoction that would soon be placed before them. When the tea arrived, they smiled at each other and sipped, trying to look as if they enjoyed it. They filled out forms electronically, the lawyer stopping after each line to check if 'Aslan' understood what she was saying. The interpreter, whose name he never found out, kept calling him *Aslam with an M*, but it made no difference to the lawyer, who clattered on her keyboard and twisted the monitor around to show them what she was writing. Aslam's discomfort escalated with each keystroke and the interpreter touched him once on his arm as if she knew. He kept his eyes lowered for the most part and decided he really did not understand English and all he knew was Urdu.

When the lawyer finished her form filling, printed them out for him to sign and went away again to make photocopies, he turned to the interpreter and told her in Urdu that he wasn't really Hazara.

'I know', she replied, also in Urdu.

'Why didn't you say something then?'

'I am an interpreter. Not an ethnicity expert.'

'But what if they find out?'

'Aslam', she said. 'You cannot worry about what you can't control. You need to eat and sleep and find some work that will sustain you. Maybe you get to stay here. Maybe not. That is in God's hands. But you deserve respect and peace. Sometimes you have to stretch the truth a little to get what you want. That's not a crime.'

'Why are they so eager for me to say I am Hazara? Where I come from, people don't say it out loud. It could get them killed.'

'Exactly. That's why it may help you stay here. If you want to stay at any cost. Consider yourself fortunate you're not in mandatory detention.' The woman lowered her voice to a whisper and Aslam shivered. Before he could stop himself, the story of Shirin and the lawyer, and nasty Janet and dear Sylvie, rushed out of him in one long monotone.

The woman touched his arm again, then continued in her normal voice, as if they were discussing the price of goat's meat at the halal butcher's. 'The real crime is locking up people and sending them to a country where they are not wanted because they are the wrong colour. Or the wrong religion. These nice white people who want to help you have never seen where our people live when we first come here. We live four to a room, sleep on mattresses on the floor and pretend we actually have enough money to pay the rent. All you have done is to grieve for that rich girl who left you in this state. And claimed the status of your ancestors.'

'Aslan?' The lawyer stood in front of him with a stack of papers. She did not look happy. Aslam thought it must be because they weren't allowed to talk in a language she didn't understand.

'For heaven's sake', the interpreter pushed her chair back and addressed the lawyer directly for the first time. 'His name is Aslam, not Aslan. How can you help him if you can't even get his name right? It's not that hard.' She patted Aslam on his arm before striding out, leaving the lawyer staring after her.

'Umm... right, Azlum, sorry about that. It is important to get the details right of course. So, it looks as if we're on our own. Your interpreter has vanished. You do read English, don't you? Let's go through all this one last time and I'll make another appointment for you.' The lawyer fiddled with the front of her low-necked shirt and Aslam looked away.

A month later Aslam was back at the centre with the same interpreter but a different lawyer. This one was a skinny young fellow with ear studs and shiny black hair. His manner was brisk, and he was confident they would have approval for Aslam to stay in the country. Yes, it was early days and all that, but he was confident. Aslam signed more forms, answered more questions about the ordeals of a Hazara-by-birth in Pakistan, admitted to being smuggled across the border as a child and prayed his devout mother would never find out how he lied. If he'd remained a believer, he would have acknowledged the Prophet's mercy all around him, because why else would complete strangers spend so much time making sure he had food, shelter, work and maybe a permanent home in this country?

The interpreter was waiting for him outside when he emerged, blinking into the December sun. She asked him if she could give him a lift and he accepted, thankful not to have to walk to the bus station in his flimsy rubber chappals or thongs, as they called them in this country.

'I can drive you home, if you like', she said.

'Oh no, the bus stop is fine. It's a long walk in this heat so...'

'It's no trouble. Really. Let me drive you home. I have a son about your age. He's also breaking his heart over a girl who doesn't care. A white girl.'

They drove silently the rest of the way. She dropped him outside the ugly red brick house in that neighbourhood he had recently begun to notice was 'dodgy' and waved him away as he stammered his thanks. He invited her in for chai and she smiled and asked if he had elaichi, then laughed at his frown as he tried to think.

'I'm only joking. I hope you do well, Aslam-Aslan. I hope you roar. Do good things. And ring your mother.'

The woman wound down the window and waved again. He remained standing on the verge where weeds met sand at the front of his share-house. Her car disappeared around the corner, and he watched the old drunk from the park lurch across the street towards him. The kids from the corner house readied themselves with water pistols in case the derelict walked past their place. The oldest kid yelled something that sounded like *effing wogs everywhere* and Aslam showed the kid his middle finger. Being sent back in disgrace to that colourful Peshawari market where his father sold embroidered topis wouldn't be such a bad thing. He turned to go inside, yelling *eff off* at the kid with the pistol.

A smell of fried garlic and chilli greeted him and the voice of Suman, their latest housemate, called out from the kitchen. He walked in to find all the housemates gathered around the girl, holding bottles of beer and clapping each other on the back. Aslam's blank look made her laugh and she said her application was through. She could live in the country as a resident Australian. Tonight, she was cooking for everyone. Tomorrow she was moving out.

'Don't look so sad, yaar.' Suman put down her spatula and hugged Aslam. 'It'll happen for you. For all of you. For us. This is the lucky country, so why shouldn't we be lucky, hey? And Aslam, you better call your mum. She rang and left a message.'

Something's Gotta Give

Sunil Badami

Two drunk girls are falling all over Spiderman, who doesn't look unhappy. Usually it's sugar-high kids, their parents looking on, kicking him in the balls or trying to pull his mask off.

It's been a quiet night, and for the first time in as long as she can remember, the great big California sky threatens rain. She hasn't made more than twenty bucks all evening.

She draws her arms together and rubs them, her eyes flicking up and down the Boulevard, rocking back on her heels. She's lucky: her spot's right in front of the Chinese Theatre, and though she's stuck next to Bogey, he's always got cigarettes.

It could be worse: Jimmy Dean is stuck on the windy corner near Vine, and he's always trembling up, his coif blown crazy, asking to bum a smoke and rest awhile out of the wind. All he gets at his star are crack addicts and stray tourists looking for the Hard Rock Café.

This is where most of the tourists gather, to gawk at the handprints in the concrete, or take photos with Spiderman or Jim Carrey as the Mask or Batman and Robin. Or her.

Most of the superheroes are college guys who've scraped together the costume. Anyone could do it: just put on a mask and strike a heroic pose. They come and go, and next year—next month—there's always someone to take their place, moving up from the darker end of the Boulevard.

The summer the last movie came out, there were four Spidermen jostling each other for prime position out front of the Chinese Theatre. Three of them got into a brawl, one being taken away in an ambulance, six teeth knocked out and blood dripping all over the suit.

The only one left, who'd ducked into Leroy's while it happened, tried to convince all the horrified children *he* was the real Spiderman and the officers were arresting the evil clones, but his breath stank like always of beer and it didn't stop their wailing or their parents' squawking as the remaining two evil clones—one whose costume had been ripped in the fracas, revealing a Satanic pentagram on his chest—were bundled into squad cars.

The wind blows stale Strip air through the palms. It pools in front of the Knitting Factory, where a bunch of goth chicks clutch their dresses down, *Seven Year Itch* style. She stamps her feet. Her knees ache.

Six Black kids are setting up a break-dancing exhibition, laying out shiny strips of cardboard and adjusting their caps. Spiderman's broken free of the college girls and flapping his wrist appreciatively as he tells the Incredible Hulk all about it. She can hear snatches: *Sweet pussy, man, sweet pussy.* College boy superheroes.

Some, like Groucho Marx and Jerry Lewis (brothers, though they don't look it), Dean Martin, Jayne Mansfield (always annoyed people confuse her with Marilyn), Bogey, her—even Michael Jackson—are the real deal: they actually look like the people they're meant to be. They're professionals: their costumes are always perfect, they always strive to keep the illusion in place.

Among the pros, it's an unspoken rule not to break character, in case there's a rube watching, waiting to take a picture for five bucks a pop, sometimes ten if you're lucky. Or if they're especially stupid.

They used to go down to Bruno's after work, scoring free drinks off the manager for keeping the 'Hollywood vibe', getting raucously drunk on slammers and shots, but she never found out Groucho's real name for ages. And he always called her Marilyn. They all did. They always do. He still makes her laugh, whatever his name is.

For a moment—Michael Jackson aside—you could imagine, in the dark smoky light of Bruno's, that Hollywood was real, that Frank and Jayne and Elvis and Marilyn and the gang were all just hanging out, living it up till they hit the next joint, living the life you'd always dreamt of. They'd blow their night's takings, comparing notes and war stories, signing autographs for star-struck drunks, who'd sometimes buy them rounds.

When she first started, the money wasn't important: she just wanted to be wonderful. She was as good as famous, almost like a real star.

She keeps looking up and down the Boulevard: there's not much traffic, just a few cabs cruising for fares, some rubes in a beat up Plymouth. It's the weather. The moment it looks like rain, everybody stays away. It's like they refuse to accept that every day couldn't be sunny. As though rain might drown the picture.

Back home, she longed for the orange sunshine, dreaming of swimming pools and convertibles, never having to worry about the smell of oily water staining her shoes.

And when she first got here, she was a kid in a candy store: she walked up and down Venice Beach in short-shorts she'd made by cutting up her old jeans, her eyes wide and her mouth open, looking for her big break.

She got sunburnt that first week: had to lie face down on Vicky's sofa, the backs of her legs raw like they'd been beaten, her stomach thick with nausea. She hadn't had the skin for this place. But once it stopped being tender, it got tougher, like it got an extra layer.

Sometimes she misses the dour weather of home, the smell of grease, wishes it would rain just once, a real flood, wash away all the exhaust fumes and the smell of suntan lotion.

But it bothers her how cold she feels now, her pores puckered and shivering, though back home this would be spring weather. She's become too used to the warmth.

Outside the bodega across the street, the bag lady is staring out the window, talking to herself again. Her eyes are milky. Two rubes walk past, their eyes on the stars on the sidewalk. One's shaking his head: 'Who the hell's Louise Brooks, anyway?' A crowd's gathering round the Black kids, waiting for something to happen.

Her feet are killing her: goddamn four-inch heels. And the corset—it feels like someone's stabbing her with switchblades. She goes through four pairs of stockings a month and at least three pairs of shoes a year. How many pairs does that make now?

Buying the first pair she thought: it's only temporary, it's better than waitressing, it'll pay the rent till I get my break, it'll be fun.

Even then she knew it wasn't true: just something she told herself to make it seem better. Just like the rubes who want to believe it really is Marilyn, *it really is*, though they know she's dead, been dead for years.

Sometimes a rube'll come up and she can tell they're thinking: *Wow, she really does look like... I wonder if she really is?* And though she giggles and blows them a kiss, she wants to say *I'm not her, I'm not! I'm someone else. Not me, exactly, but not her.*

Sometimes she wonders if she really is who she says she is. Not when she's in the dress blowing kisses, but when she's home, and kicked off the heels and unlaced the corset and hung the dress for the next day and scrubbed her face till it's red and shiny and raw and still, no matter how hard she tries, the same as *hers*. As always, as long as she can remember.

Nobody ever told her she was pretty when she was a little girl. But one night, when her mum was still at work, Bo came into her room and put his hand on her leg, letting it rest there till her thigh got hot and itchy under the sheet, a sick feeling rising in her stomach. His tongue was slick with beer as it snaked out from under his moustache, wet and lazy. 'Yew know who yew look lahk?...'

How many times has she heard it since? As though she'd never noticed, brushing her teeth or applying her makeup or catching a glimpse of her face in the shiny glass of the boutiques on Rodeo, full of beautiful things she knows more and more now she'll never afford.

Once, her eyes'd've sparkled; once, she'd've felt a blooming pride. Now, she feels anything but.

The wind flicks a curl into her eyes, and she sweeps it up, tucking it into her hair. The Black kids have started their beatbox up, and its heavy, fuzzy beat spits out across the Boulevard. The crowd around them has started to thicken, clapping along as she catches glimpses of red or orange tracksuited legs flipping out over the tops of their heads.

That's not good, especially for Spiderman and the Incredible Hulk, talking to each other out of the sides of their mouths as they eye the crowd. It's creating a bottleneck, which also means she and the rest of the pros, up the La Brea end, will miss out on steady traffic coming up from the east.

'Lucky?' asks Bogey, flicking the cigarettes one-two out of a silver case. Sure. She hunches into the lighter, though the flame flickers in the wind. It takes her a couple of tries to get lit. When she exhales, the smoke flutters up to the Strip in a long translucent ribbon.

She looks at him, properly for the first time, she thinks. He doesn't look like Bogey, but if you closed your eyes, you'd think it was him. When she first got her spot, right next to him, she'd ask him over and over to say, 'Play it again, Sam'. He'd protest that wasn't the line, but she'd plead and flirt till he relented. 'Play it again, Sam, play it again.'

Once, stumbling out of Bruno's, he'd taken her to his bungalow off the 101, decked out in thirties furniture and old film posters. He flicked the cigarettes one-two out of the silver case. They drank scotch from crystal tumblers. 'Here's lookin' at you, kid', he said, and she blushed: she couldn't remember any lines. Then he kissed her.

They were still in their costumes, and she caught sight of them in the living room mirror, the cigarettes burning down into the ashtray. It looked just like a movie, and when she closed her eyes, she was someone else, somewhere else, somehow something she'd always imagined.

The next morning, trying to shake the smoke out of the dress where she'd left it on the floor, she heard him clear his throat in the bathroom and ask in a Joisey accent if she'd like some *kawfee*. She left without speaking, without shutting the front door.

Things had been awkward for a while. She could feel him looking at her, but she didn't acknowledge him. She tensed a little when some rubes asked for a photo of them together, but they paid fifteen bucks, so she put up with his hands pressing into her hip.

Now they've reached a kind of polite distance. He'll still flick her cigarettes one-two out of the silver case.

At least he has another voice. People think she's staying in character, but this is the way she speaks. There are rumours Michael Jackson's spent twenty grand to look like Michael Jackson, even had his larynx scraped, but she's never had that choice. She's always looked like this, sounded like this, like someone else. Always has, and sometimes it frightens her she always will.

The Black kids are arguing over whose turn it is next, and the crowd is starting to wander. Spiderman and the Incredible Hulk snap to attention, striking heroic poses at passers-by. She tramples her cigarette, feels the nicotine tingle. Her wrists throb.

She'd done a few auditions when she'd first got here, through an agent Vicky knew. But after all the waiting, all the hoping, she began to suspect it was hopeless. 'You know who you look like', they'd say, and that was the end of that. Sometimes she didn't even get a chance to say anything.

The agent sent her to try out for the lead in a Marilyn biopic, nothing big, just TV, but they wanted a 'name'. You look too much like her, they'd said, as though that was all there was to acting. In the end, they'd given it to an unknown. It disappeared without trace.

After that, she thought about plastic surgery: they wanted thin girls now. But she could never go through with it, even if she could've afforded it. She was too afraid of who she'd become.

There was a girl Vicky knew in their building who'd started doing porn. *Adult entertainment*, she called it, though that didn't seem the right description. She'd had the works, and it looked like they'd sucked everything out of her bottom half and stuffed it into the top. She called herself Destiny: it sounded *classy*, she said.

She teetered over to their apartment and asked in an old voice if she could learn how to talk like Marilyn. The girly voice. This is the way I always speak, she'd said, and the girl smirked as far as her lips would allow. Still, she let her imitate her for a couple of hours, even though it felt like she was being sent up. She got tired of hearing everything repeated back at her.

'Let's just talk, okay?' *'Let's just talk, okay?'* 'Stop repeating everything.' *'Stop repeating everything.'*

One night Vicky came home with Destiny's latest video.

They got drunk on white wine and giggled as they made up stupid porn film titles before they put it on. *Beverley Hills 9021-Ho. The Sperminator. Star Whores.* The film wasn't as imaginative. The lighting was terrible, the camera work jerky, and they couldn't hear anything over the tape hiss. Destiny didn't speak: she serviced two big Black guys by a pool, her head bobbing up and down to organ music. She had a distant look in her eyes and her moans sounded overdubbed. There were dead leaves in the pool.

She wondered what'd make you decide you'd do porn—not just blowing strangers in a cheap house in the Valley, but giving up on the big break. The whole world knowing. Vicky said a thousand bucks a scene. How'd she know that? Vicky smiled, but said nothing.

Watching two Latina hookers in shiny hot pants make their way from the Strip to the bodega across the road, she thinks about all the Marilyn movies with porny titles: *Let's Make Love*, *Gentlemen Prefer Blondes*, *Some Like it Hot*...

A Chinese man with a bag full of counterfeit DVDs passes wordlessly through the crowd. He stashes them as two squad cars turn up in front of the Chinese Theatre, their sirens flashing.

The cops break up the remains of the crowd around the Black kids. They surround one of the kids, leaning over him as the dispatch crackles from one of the cars. One of them has his hands on his hips, brushing his gun. Four of the kids are arguing with the cops, but one is off to the side, counting the money and packing up the cardboard strips. He looks up at her, then back at the cops and the other kids, then back at her, and shrugs.

She looks up the Boulevard; first, the La Brea end to the hazy lights of the Strip, the neon expanding out of the hills. Then, back down the block to Las Palmas, where the lights run out at the corner past Musso and Frank's. She's hungry. Maybe when Vicky gets here they'll head down to Roscoe's for some chicken and waffles, but now all she wants is a taco. A soft taco.

She turns to Bogey to see if he wants anything. She won't owe him, even for a smoke. He's standing close to Jayne Mansfield as she brushes lint off his tux.

A cop is putting handcuffs on the Black kid while the other barks Miranda. 'You have the right to remain silent.' The kid looks dead already. Rubes slow as they walk past, their eyes wide, whispering into their hands. 'Nothing to see, move along.'

As she's about to cross the street, a rube comes up. She can tell he's been looking at her for some time: the expectant face, the nervous smile. She sets her face, waiting for the inevitable. *Yew know who yew look lahk?* He approaches. A photo? She giggles. Photos *are* a girl's best friend! The emptiness in her stomach rises up. Only fifteen dollars!

The rube looks at her like he's trying to work out who she is. She's confused. He tilts his head to one side, his eyes narrowing.

'Yew look lahk...' She smiles, nodding her head in encouragement. 'Somebody ah used to know. A gehl. Lori Mae?' She gulps. Nobody calls her that. 'Lori Mae Mynor?'

'I'm—I'm Marilyn Monroe, honey.' 'Yew look lahk...' Her laugh falters. 'Maybe you...'

His eyes glint down the Boulevard. Groucho and Jerry are doing their routine, though nobody's buying. It's late, and some, like Spiderman, are already packing up.

She doesn't recognise him. That frightens her. The rubes all look alike to her. He comes closer, his voice thick with peanuts. He looks pleased, his tongue darting out of his lips with excitement. 'Don't yew remembah? Ah always sayd yew looked lahk...'

And then she does remember.

He looks much older without his moustache. 'What're yew doing here?'

'Well, I didn't want to be looked for.'

His tongue slips out before he can catch it. He pulls her to him, his fingers oily.

'Whatcha think you're doing?'

Behind them, Bogey is flicking cigarettes out one-two for Jayne Mansfield, and Michael Jackson is twirling to himself. A skiddering feeling swells inside. 'Leave me alone!' Everybody looks up, and one of the cops taking statements puts his hand to his gun and starts to walk over. 'I want to be left alone!'

Bo's eyebrows knit together in confusion. 'Now, don't be lahk theyt, Lori Mae...'

'Ah ain't Lori Mae, ah'm—'

She pushes him away and runs across the street. A cab screeches in front of her. *Stupid bitch! Look where ya goin'!* She gives him the finger, runs across the Boulevard to the Roosevelt, her heels clattering on the stars. The air's heavy: it's going to rain.

When she first got here, she moved into an apartment she couldn't afford in the Las Palmas Hotel. They'd filmed *Pretty Woman* there. The Hollywood sign shimmered in the hills and when she painted her nails on the fire escape she'd watch the letters dance in the haze. Sometimes she thought of all the thousands of girls sitting alone like her, dreaming of becoming a star. But she'd just dream harder.

She read everything she could about Marilyn, watched all the movies. She walked and talked and sang like her. Once, drunk, she'd slept on the lawn outside the Brentwood house where she'd died, till the owner turned on the sprinklers. She'd go sit in her dark booth in the corner of the bar at the Roosevelt, smiling when drunk businessmen tried it on. She so wanted to be her then it hurt.

And then after all the rejections and unreturned calls, she grew her hair out, dyed it black. She got a nose stud, wore too much kohl, got a stupid tattoo on the Strip when she was drunk again. Big bust, big ass, big deal.

No matter what she did, they'd always say the same thing. The agent stopped booking her. She looked too much like her to be herself. She got evicted, and when Vicky took her in, all she had left was fifty cents and the dress. She cried her eyes out on the couch for a week.

Then one night she got a fifth of vodka and drove up to the Griffith Observatory. She got out of the car and picked her way down the cliff face through the scrub and stones. She sat on a rock in the dress and drank till there was nothing left. She'd been here a couple of times before with the old Jimmy Dean.

The old Jimmy Dean had been working at a McDonald's in Saint Paul, Minnesota, when they'd cast him in an ad where he walked down Times Square in a raincoat like James Dean, eating a cheeseburger. The estate sued and the ad got pulled. The old Jimmy Dean had tried to make it over here, but it was the same old story.

Once they'd gone up to the Observatory and watched the city lights bleed into the stars. He didn't know what else to do.

He couldn't go back to Minnesota. But he didn't know where to go next. He didn't know who he was anymore. When she pulled him to her, he seemed startled. They didn't talk the rest of that long night.

A few weeks later, he disappeared. Like he'd fallen off the face of the earth. The new Jimmy Dean took his place, though he always looked nervous, like the old Jimmy Dean might come back. But he never did.

Perched on the rock in the dress and heels, she thought about all the whats and hows and whys. Nothing really made sense. The light lines mapping out the city became fuzzy and she felt cold. And needed a smoke. She'd left her jacket in the car, but when she'd tried to walk back up in the heels, she slipped. She slid down the cliff face; the dress shredded like torn-off skin.

She came to in a terrible stillness before dawn, covered in thorns and bruises. She had to climb up the cliff back to the car before anybody found her. It was painful and she tore all her nails. She didn't think she'd make it. When she got to the rock, she threw up the vodka. It splashed all over her and trickled in sticky trails in the dust. She couldn't go on. But somehow she made it back to the car and drove home.

Vicky looked horrified, and when she tried to brush the gravel out of her hair, it was spattered with blood. Vicky washed her and put her to bed with a sleeping pill. She didn't know how long she slept, or what she'd dreamt, or if she'd dreamt at all, but when she woke, she felt like a different person. She couldn't go on. She didn't want to go back, didn't know where to go next, but she just couldn't go on. What was left?

Vicky promised her things would get better. She'd see what she could do. She couldn't give up now. 'Just a little longer. You'll see.'

Everything's quiet in the Roosevelt. It's brown like an old photo. There's a mirror near the elevator which used to hang in Marilyn's suite. They say you can see her apparition in it if you look hard enough. She sways there, not seeing the rubes walking around her with astonished faces as they head up for the night. All she sees is someone else, bruises on her arms.

A hand on her shoulder, and she turns round, startled. Vicky. 'I thought I'd find you here. I was held up. What happened?' She bursts into hollow sobs that curdle the Muzak. She pushes her face into Vicky's breast, while Vicky coos. 'Hush now. Don't cry, baby. Vicky's here. Everything's gonna be all right.'

'Yew promise?'

Vicky holds her face in her hands. 'I saw *the man*.'

She looks up and wipes the tears away. 'What'd he say?'

'He said he wants to meet you. He's interested. Very interested.'

'What's he want me to do again?'

Vicky smiles, but says nothing.

Strange Days

Heterochromia Iridum

Niharika Chibber Joe and Matthew M. Lupton

At 2.04 AM somewhere in the United States, two sets of insomnia-ridden thumbs rapidly conveyed truncated sentiments speedily over dimly lit screens. Their fingers had long forgotten how to properly hold pens, sleep was elusive, and the mind raced. The pandemic was taking its toll on these unlikely buddies. They had been neighbours, but it was the pandemic that had brought them together on a shared screen, where they traded their imaginations, exchanged barbs, swapped pithy quotes, shared haunting music, and proffered wisecracks that helped keep the other from jumping off the proverbial ledge. 'So, buddy', said Thumb Set 1, 'Can't sleep?' 'No', responded Thumb Set 2, 'I am burned out.' 'All right then', Thumb Set 1 texted, 'See where you can go with this!'

It was a cool, not yet frigid amber evening in early November 1990. The twenty-nine-year-old walked out of her cold office at the faceless conglomerate with exactly eight dollars in her pocket and a mood to match. It had been another goddamned long day, and all she could look forward to was going home to turning thirty at midnight; a cat that couldn't have cared less; a motley assortment of books; and a busted television set that could still manage, in black and white, horrors from around the world. And who the heck knew what lurked in the fridge with its flickering light!

Hungry, emotionally starved, physically exhausted, she realised all she could afford were a package of instant ramen noodles, perhaps a few veggies, and some tea to wind her down. Carrying her eight dollars and her bruised self to the corner bodega in search of calories and a flimsy pretext to avoid going home, she found herself lackadaisically thumbing through cramped aisles.

Her head buzzing with the frequency of the fluorescent flycatcher overhead, she weighed the consequences of tomato versus corn soup. 'What the hell am I doing with my life?' she chastised herself inwardly. 'I could have been a hero! What has happened to me?! I should never have taken that train to Cincinnati!' Fighting the familiar internal battle, she wound her way down her tangents and cans of tomato soup, inadvertently knocking over a few that went clattering obnoxiously down the aisle. A truant rolling can collided with a leather boot a few feet away, and brown eyes met blue, and rested.

Thumb Set 2's thumbs were now flying, and Thumb Set 1 returned the volleys as they came in.

A shared moment of silence, and Leather Boot gently inquired, 'Wanna trade eyeballs? Just one for one? I've been yearning to see the world through different eyes. Mine can't distinguish borders, horizons or ephemeral values anymore. And yours are just so very pretty. They appear to have seen so much, yet carry such innocence. Let's trade! I'll let you see the world out of my left orbit. It's the good one. It has excellent aim, and I use it to shoot.'

Soup Girl stood there looking at him absently. Not shocked, not afraid, just trying to make sense of the familiarity the situation presented. She was intrigued. 'Sure', she responded. 'How about my Left for yours? But riddle me this, Leather Boot, how am I to know that thing inside your head hasn't seen things that I haven't already seen? Will I see your flashbacks? Your hidden bloody moments? Stars, but not substance? Can you promise me a good time with that eye?'

'Oh, my dear girl', sighed Leather Boot, unclenching his sweaty palms to pop out his Left. 'You need a break. Don't look now, but I'm gonna PayPal you 18.5 million dollars. It should land in a few minutes. Go take a trip and get the hell outta dodge for a few months. Get some proper food, do your hair, get your health back. The safest way to travel these days is by private train car. Will that be agreeable?' Soup Girl hesitated, accepted the Left, and completed the swap. 'Let me know when you send the money.' A few uncomfortable moments passed in silence as they adjusted their left orbits. 'I'm waiting', she finally announced. 'Seems like the connection is slow. Are the funds coming via a Nigerian prince?'

'Ah, that's right', exclaimed Leather Boot, smacking the right side of his head to settle his newest left orb. 'I've gotta call my guy in the Seychelles. He does my bitcoin mining, on a 1,200-acre server farm on an oil rig. International waters, no laws, you see! Ping might be lagging. Servers get buggy when you push them too hard for five years straight.'

'Ping is certainly lagging', Soup Girl grumbled, trying to push the uncooperative orb back into its inhospitable new cradle. 'As it turns out, Ping is my guy in New Zealand. He's the result of a one-night stand between a Han Chinese businessman and a Macanese prostitute. Even though he presents as Chinese, growing up in the red-light district of Macau made him the object of ridicule. Not to mention his heterochromia iridum. Y'know, different coloured eyeballs? Not that there's anything wrong with that. They look cool, if I may say so myself. In any case, at seventeen, Ping stowed away on the hydrofoil to Hong Kong, where a stranger he met in a dark alley offered him a job as a spot boy on the set of a James Bond film. Fast forward twenty years, and Ping is a rotund financier living in Auckland, where he counts his cryptocurrency carefully. The problem is, when he was a boy, Ping took a smack to the head from his mother's pimp. He's never been quite right since then. That's why Ping is lagging.'

Meanwhile, watching his brother's finance career closely from afar, Pong smiled gently from the balcony of his Stockholm penthouse. He'd hoped to contact Ping soon, having recently learned of his twin's existence. Separated so shortly after birth, Ping and Pong had never known the other existed. The newborn Pong had been sold by his mother to pay down hefty debts from an ill-fated chinchilla farm start-up in Macau. The fabulously wealthy, classically beautiful, yet humble fairy that lived in the wild woods of northern Sweden bought Pong, and raised him alone. But before separating him from his twin, she used a painless spell to exchange Ping's amber left eye for Pong's left blue one. At the time, it seemed like a keepsake for each brother; but neither their concubine mother, her pimp, nor their businessman father knew why, leaving Ping and Pong to deal with their heterochromia in their own ways.

Pong's adoptive fairy mother proved to be a wonderful soul, cherishing and loving him, if not a bit smothering on occasion. As a boy, Pong became a fan of the 1938 *Snow White*. He also developed a keen interest in all things machines. Pong spent his childhood traipsing through the woods and the wild. He often stumbled upon the fresh corpse of a recently deceased owl or baby brown bear. He would bring them home. Then, by employing his fledgling aptitude in alchemy, taxidermy and mechanical engineering, he would resurrect them, turning them into well-spirited friends. Not quite dead. Not quite wholly magical, or even sentient automatons; but creatures that loved him without question. Pong was an only-lonely child, and these were the only friends he had. The few other boys and girls he did meet by chance during his forest roamings were at first excited to see this creature with the multicoloured eyes in the woods. But they invariably ran away screaming, with vomit on their shirts, in fear of the ungodly machines following poor Pong so closely, with their clanking and vented steam. Half rusting, half rotting.

By the time he found himself brooding at Oxford, Pong finally understood his odd vision flashes. Scenes from someone else's life would override the vision in his left eye, his current reality still seen plain in his right. Someone with hands very much like his own, typing at a desk, reading what looked to be a Kiwi newspaper, stroking the hair of some nameless pretty woman. They were vignettes from *another life*. They were not dreams, nor the subconscious in reflux. Nothing else made sense.

One decade, a successful marriage and a dozen just-as-successful multi-corporations later, Pong finally unravelled his Great Mystery at the age of thirty. This had to be someone born of the same womb. He came to the realisation sitting in his office while working on revolutionising the doorbell industry by skipping the whole electricity mess and ear-shattering bells and updating the software of his mass-produced, made-to-order animal creations. Sitting there, the vision visited him again, and through his brother's left eye he saw what Ping, the financier, had seen during the climax of the latest James Bond film, *Baron Von Blonde Bondage*. Left eye watching 007 drawing his Walther PPK to dispassionately deliver a round to the heart of his love interest turned current nemesis.

It was then that Pong finally knew, and was in equal parts overjoyed and pensive. Now, on his penthouse balcony with a sweeping view of the city of Stockholm, sucking on a clove cigarette with cognac in hand, Pong daydreamed of merging brands with his soon-to-be-found twin.

The Thumb Sets were getting sleepy. Their collective imaginations were tapped out. Soup Girl found herself sitting on the floor of the bodega. The overhead fly catcher was still buzzing a neon blue, and the large clock above it quietly indicated midnight.

Her new orb burned a distracting itch, her head was resting on Leather Boot's shoulder, and both her legs had fallen asleep. She fidgeted, and sat up. 'Wait!' she exclaimed. 'Did you just show us our future?' 'No', he sighed, stroking her hair. His newly heterochromatic eyes half shut. 'That was our past. Our future starts now. Happy birthday, Soup Girl!'

The Scent of the Ocean

Susanne Gervay

She showered and washed her hair with her Dead Sea shampoo. The scent of the ocean swept over her like rolling waves. She hated dirty hair. Her mother used to wash her flossy brown hair when she was small, making her feel warm, clean. Smoothing out the blanket, Sylvia grimaced at the neatly made bed. She fingered the neat row of 'candy' on the side table, beside Jane Austen's *Pride and Prejudice.* Closing the book, she pressed on its cover. No more study of Jane Austen for her final exams. No more analysis of the hero, Mr Darcy. There was no hero for her in those pages.

Her father looked like a hero with his dark hair and swaggering gait. He called her 'princess'. She loved that name. She did not love him on those nights he came home smelling of scotch and strange women's perfume. He'd argue with her mother. Then, Sylvia covered her little sister's ears and held her closely. Sylvia held the scotch bottle like a lover. She swallowed. It was empty now. She lay on her neat bed.

The woman was familiar. Her mother? Her auburn hair belied her age. She was shaking Sylvia out of her sleep, hurting her, forcing Sylvia to open her eyes.

'Leave me... alone... alone.' Sylvia moved between consciousness and unconsciousness.

A uniformed man lifted her from her bed making her see that it was untidy now. Her mother wouldn't like that. She fought. 'I hate you.'

But the movement away continued and more men in uniforms carried her. She didn't hear the sirens, and they pumped scotch and pills from her stomach.

It hurt. Hurt. Everything hurt.

Her mother brought her a nightie in the hospital. Sylvia buried her face in the pillow.

'How could you do this to us? To yourself?' her mother cried.

Sylvia buried her face in the sheet under the pillow. She did not want guilt. She wanted out. 'Bitch.'

'What, Sylvia?'

Her daughter did not answer.

Her father came. Really, her parents should have modelled for a detergent advertisement, the way they did with their Facebook photos. They wore smart casual clothes, smiled, held hands with their princesses beside them. They were perfect. 'Why did you do it, Sylvia? What's wrong?'

Didn't they know? She didn't want to see the lies behind infidelities. A black man shot seven times in the back. In America, by the police, with his three kids watching. She did not want starvation flashed across her phone beside the Kardashians with their fake bodies. Couldn't they let her alone? But they forced her back.

She was enraged. Sylvia screamed. 'Get out. It's your fucking fault.'

Her father wanted to hit her. The mother grabbed him, pushing him towards the door and Sylvia felt relieved. She did not want to feel at all.

She saw that her father would never forget the attack. His love for her became tainted with a permanent anger.

Her father visited every day forcing time between work and phone calls. Her mother brought her seven-year-old sister to the hospital. She was happy to see Sylvia and Sylvia tried to be happy for her. Her little sister did not understand, yet. Their father called her his little princess. Sylvia did not want her to become like her.

The doctors interrogated Sylvia. 'What do you feel about your parents?'

'What do you feel about yours?' Sylvia lit up an imaginary cigarette. No cigarettes were allowed in the nut ward.

'Sylvia, you are not cooperating. We want to help you.'

She kept thinking. Why? Why? She demanded, 'Then let me out of here.'

'We will as soon as you are well.'

'So you think I am sick?' Sylvia half-enjoyed the game. It was better than the pointless deadness of the hospital.

'You tried to kill yourself, didn't you? What do you think?'

She shrugged. 'Just drank too much and you know how adolescents like to experiment with drugs.'

The doctors wrote down: *uncooperative*. 'See you tomorrow then.'

'Do I have a choice?' Sylvia walked past the other nuts in the waiting room—the kids who were anorexic, schizophrenic, cutting themselves, fracturing between what was real and in their heads.

Her friends visited. They were nice but awkward, not sure what to say to Sylvia. Her parents had asked them what happened at school. Nothing happened. That was just the point. Mediocre teachers set rules and became heads of subjects, while the good ones plodded on, frustrated, unfulfilled, moving on after a while.

Sylvia had organised a passive resistance strike. Gandhi would have been proud. His words were seared into her mind. *The future depends on what you do today.* Their history teacher, Mrs Thomas dictated endless boring notes in a monologue on the history of Indian and Pakistani independence in 1947. Hindu India. Islamic Pakistan. Partition of two countries. Democracy. Congratulations. She did not read out the notes on communities that had coexisted for nearly a millennium attacking each other in terrifying violence, with Hindus and Sikhs on one side and Muslims on the other, in a mutual genocide. She did not read the notes on villages aflame, on men, women and children hacked to death. Sylvia closed her eyes, blocking out today's news flash of three children on the Indian-Pakistani border. The little boy's eyes were fragmented like shards of glass. The baby sucked his fingers, his black eyes like olive pips. Their big sister stood beside them. She always looked after them, but her princess eyes were vacant. Their father lay dead on the bed behind them.

Mrs Thomas was the great pretender. Pretending to pass on the truth of the past, which was true, or half true or a lie or distorted or fake. She instructed the class, 'Girls, open your books.'

The girls looked at Sylvia. She gave them the nod. The girls crossed their arms and lay their heads down on their desks. Some girls copied everyone because they were sheep. Others hated Mrs Thomas's deadly dull history lessons. Others thought it was heroic and imagined themselves standing on desks like in *Dead Poets Society*. Some were Sylvia's friends. Some wanted truth, so they could think and act for the future.

'Lift your heads up.' No one moved. 'Look at me', Mrs Thomas demanded.

But nails were already embedded in the girls' hands. They could not move. Would not move.

Mrs Thomas's eyes shot misguided cannonballs at the heads of the girls. 'Open your books.'

'No.' Sylvia's word echoed through the room.

Mrs Thomas started to march between the desks.

'It is a sin to kill history.' Sylvia's words were soft, like a velvet glove. Every head turned towards Sylvia.

Mrs Thomas stopped. A nervous flush spread across her face. Turning on her heels, she thundered out of the classroom.

The principal was a jerk and demanded an apology from Sylvia. She refused and Sylvia was suspended. Her parents tried to understand, argued, then forced her to conform. Sylvia apologised to Mrs Thomas. She felt a bitter disappointment to the girls in her class. To the three children in the news flash, with broken eyes standing at their father's bed. To her parents. Her sister. Herself.

Those endless sessions with the doctors continued. Once she revealed to them that it was too hard being her parents' daughter. 'My mother cries at night. I hear her, but she pretends everything is all right. And daddy comes home late with lipstick on his collar.' Sylvia laughed at the cliché. 'They are liars, really.' Sylvia saw the doctors look at each other, satisfied with themselves. She felt tricked. She didn't want to play their game. So she played her own and never told them anything again.

She overheard an assessment about her.

'We are getting nowhere with Sylvia.'

'So, what do you think?'

'She may do it again. We have to put her on medication. No choice.'

She felt insane as she escaped from the hospital, waiting for the locked ward door to be left ajar. Skimming down the corridors and through the glass entrance doors, she raced up the main street, past the shops and over the pedestrian crossing. People stared. Panting, she stopped in an alleyway. She took out her phone and rang her girlfriend. 'I've got to get out.' Her friend told her to go back. But why? Where? How? Sylvia looked at her nightie. Her mother had washed it as usual. She was a saint and she would agree with the doctors. They were gods, you know. They would decide her life. But they did not know her. Where could she go anyway? She knew she had to get discharged, and her feet moved back towards the ward. Just play the game.

'I realised you're right. I want to get well.' Sylvia lied like her parents, her school, the news, the dancing teacher who put his hands between her legs.

She knew she wasn't sick. It was them. She couldn't understand why they thought it was worthwhile. Didn't they know the Arctic was melting into the sea? Islands were sinking into the Pacific. Oceans were choking on plastic and garbage. Didn't they see the news, Facebook, Insta, TikTok?

Yes, I love my parents.

Yes, I'm sorry I hurt them.

Yes, I am lucky to have a family.

Yes, I want to go to school.

Yes, I agree. I agree. Always agree.

Yes, I am a cabbage.

The doctors nodded. They were cabbages too. Sylvia laughed and the doctors approved.

She packed her bag. Her mother was scared of her now. It irritated Sylvia. Her father hugged her too hard. She was allowed to go home. Thank god. There were mad people in the ward.

She went to college to re-do her last year of school. No one minded when she walked out of classes or pierced her belly button. She passed her exams brilliantly. Her father wanted her to study law.

'Your room is a mess, Sylvia.'

'Jesus, can't I have any space? It is my room.'

'Do not blaspheme. It is my house. Clean your room.'

Sylvia left her mother standing there. She slammed the front door and walked to her friend's place. She hated hurting her mother. It was a relief to lie on a couch and drink too much. She went to a lecture on God. The Catholic priest argued with her about theology and she tried to tell him life was more than Catholicism. God was in them all. That there were many faiths. Many pathways. 'How can we live, if your way is the only way?' He did not hear her.

Sylvia was religious but her soul felt sick, so she took cocaine and wore the cross her parents had given her at confirmation.

University was interesting. Her father was angry when she chose psychology, not law. She experimented with mice. They'd run round and round hoping for food. But the food only came intermittently and they ran and ran hoping to find it, because they remembered.

The lecturer said she had to finish the experiment, but how could she? The repeated stupidity of the mice trapped in a rigid pattern of expectation horrified her. The mice kept running. One desperate mouse just collapsed in exhaustion.

She didn't know why she went out with Anthony. He didn't care about climate change. But he was good-looking, except for his lips. They were too big, voluptuous, and her stomach turned a little. He was ten years older than her and had his own law firm. He was charming like her father. Sylvia's parents thought he would keep her safe. They approved.

It was challenging when he kissed her with his loose lips. She ran to the bathroom and washed her mouth. At least soap tasted real, not like the lie of their relationship. He took her to the best restaurants and asked her to marry him.

At breakfast, she cried over yesterday's news and her father asked, 'What's wrong?'

She turned her phone towards him. 'They torture people in camps in China. The Uyghurs.'

'They're Islamic.' He shrugged and closed his newspaper. 'Anyway, who knows if it is true.'

'You can see it's true. See the photos.'

'Could still be a lie. You're lucky we live here.' Impatiently, he drank his coffee. Looked at the time. He had an early morning work meeting.

Sylvia ran all the way to the preschool. In her psychology degree, she had to report observations of children's behaviour. She nodded at the preschool director and sat cross-legged on the floor. She slipped out her notebook. Kids were clambering all over the cardboard castle. She smiled at their games. Everyone was in costume. A prince with his cut-out crown was standing like a lord at the top. He had thrown a ball to the knights building a foam moat. They threw the ball back. Three fairies were making Play-Doh party cakes. A girl was sitting alone in her princess dress. The kids played around her, as if she wasn't there. They shouted to each other, over and around her. Sylvia shuffled next to the princess. She took out two caramels from her pocket. Popped one into her mouth. The princess copied. Sylvia put her hand over the princess's hand. She would not marry Anthony.

Sylvia wrote in her notebook. 'Princess scared. *I am scared.*' She told the teacher that the princess was in trouble.

'She's just shy. Her parents told me that. She's fine.' She turned to the busyness of end-of-day exits. Parents, grandparents, carers, children were running for their bags and looking for lost things as they were signed out of the preschool. When Sylvia left, the princess's eyes followed her.

'I'll be back for you.' Sylvia smiled at her, but her heart was sore. She whispered, 'I want to save princesses.'

The afternoon was balmy. She put in her earphones and switched on her phone. There were messages.

'Sorry about our argument. I shouldn't go into your room. Made your favourite crumbed fish tonight. Waiting for you for dinner. Your sister made you a special card. See you at home. Love you always.' Mum.

'Hey, we're making *Stop Climate Change* signs for the Saturday march. My place. Thursday 6 PM. Bring cardboard & stuff. I got the pizza. Everyone's coming. So you have to be there. It'll be fun.'

'Got tickets to the theatre. Call me.' Anthony.

News feeds pinged on her phone. Sexual abuse. Trump. Budgets. Terrorist trials. 50% off large pizzas. Facebook. Insta. Twitter. Her head was exploding. Sylvia switched off her phone.

The scent of the ocean swept over her like rolling waves. She walked to the beach. The chill in the air had left the beach deserted. Sandstone cliffs cut into the blueness of the dark sea, with the setting sun giving a scarlet backdrop. Sylvia gasped at the beauty of it. The cool sand between her toes made her shiver. Sylvia left her backpack with her notes and phone on the sand. She did not need it anymore. The sea called her. Breathless, she charged into the water, her T-shirt clinging to her as if pasted on. Her skirt flapping in the currents, wrapping around her legs. Swimming, swimming, she reached beyond the waves.

As she closed her eyes, her body began to tingle, the cold reaching deep into her bones. The glorious feeling of letting go consumed her, as she sank further and further towards the seabed. Her eyelids fluttered open as the water rippled above her. There were no lies there. No distorted truths. She breathed in and out, embracing the release. It was a beautiful surrender.

She did not know when the salt water began to burn her throat. When her little sister's hands reached out to her through the ripples. When she started gurgling, choking, coughing, thrashing. When she reached for myriad figures, her mother, the preschool princess, the children out there who were not mice. The baby boy on a faraway border with olive pip eyes and his dead father behind him.

Sylvia rose, as if from the dead. Up and up and up until she saw the sandstone cliffs bathed in the rays of scarlet sunset. Gasping, air filled her lungs. Her short breaths became longer, her heart beat less quickly. Her body stopped fighting. Calmly, she lay on her back, with her arms outstretched like a cross. The waves in an unstoppable rhythm took her back to the shore.

The future depends on what you do today. Gandhi.

Learning to Bake

Janhavi Acharekar

The breeze brought in the pungent smell of drying fish, as it did those days. Windows opened to reveal a washed-out blue sky. Bluer than the one remembered from their childhood, perhaps. But childhood had been some time ago and memories can be elusive.

The ocean is a blob. It reflects the colours of the sky to a cliché, encircling the bobbing fishing boats in swirling strokes. It echoes the shrill whistling of the kites as they glide through the warm currents, slowly at first, and then dementedly, threatening to swoop towards the open window—an inch closer than the previous day—only to take a sharp turn and fly away into the horizon again.

They paint in silence all day. A cyclist goes by, one hand fidgeting with his face covering before adjusting his crotch. Hours later, two women with shopping bags walk past, oblivious to the egret hunched over the edge of the promenade.

He lights a cigarette from his fast diminishing reserve, resting an elbow on the windowsill. His eyes rest on the neighbour's garden, a rarity in a city like theirs.

'You could smell the grass from their lawn this morning', she says. 'Made me long for the hills.'

The pavement dwellers get into a fight, only to behave themselves when the police jeep drives past, on its languorous round at noon.

Aat raha. Stay indoors, instructs the sub-inspector on the loudspeaker, going on to elucidate the ill effects of disobeying orders in the wake of a pandemic.

The street children stand to attention, listening carefully. *Stay indoors*, they seem to mouth, bursting into giggles and wrestling each other to the ground as soon as the jeep turns the corner.

'I'll make us some sandwiches for lunch', she says, making her way to the kitchen.

'I'll cook dinner later', he promises, distractedly, training his gaze on a pizza delivery boy being stopped from entering the building.

They lapse into silence and then congregate again to observe the sunset at six. He dials his father.

'Too many patients, son. Too many. And the nurses are too few', says the voice at the other end.

'Yes, dad', he sighs. 'I know.'

'Let's speak tomorrow, okay? I need to tend to a new patient in five minutes. Emphysema. Twenty-one years old.'

'Okay. Let's speak tomorrow', he replies, and hangs up.

She puts her arm around his waist. They gaze at the ball of fire in the sea. The illusion of tongues of flames leaping through the waters in the shape of a ring; a trick played by the sun.

And in this manner, the day stretches into a yawn. The silence and solitude in the metropolis are new. The isolation, not so much.

The next day is no different. He attends a few calls. She speaks with her mother. In a repetition of the previous day's routine, they chat by the window occasionally, and then separate to tend to their works of art.

The pavement dwellers are huddled together in a group under a copperpod—the lone deciduous tree amid a queue of toddy palms and coconut trees swaying at a distance of a few feet from each other like a socially distanced line of people outside a grocery store.

The street children ride a colourful tricycle at noon, three on a seat, oblivious to the arrival of the oppressive summer heat. The older boys play a game with stones. The women wear colourful saris—magenta, parrot green, purple with gold and silver piping—as if the onus of bringing cheer into their lives rests on their own shoulders.

Two men on a scooter cause the group to scatter. Their rudimentary kerchief-masks give them the appearance of bandits; but to the pavement dwellers, they are Samaritans who distribute rice and biscuits. The younger siblings fight over the biscuits.

He calls his sister and she assures him that all is well.

'Does dad get his meals on time?' he asks. She affirms that he does, adding that the nurses are lovely.

Today, the blue sky reminds him of doctors' scrubs. The white clouds, of nurses in uniform.

'Are you done, daddy? I'm waiting to have dinner with you, okay?' a high-pitched, little boy's voice from the distant past surfaces from the recesses of his mind.

His earliest memories were of waiting for his father to get done with the last patient. Of acquainting himself with names of medical conditions like bronchiectasis and pleural effusion at the end of the day, when his father returned from the hospital. Of being invited by the nurses for the cutting of his father's birthday cake, the numerals changing from thirty-five to seventy-five in a flash. For as long as he could remember, his father had tirelessly met the demands of the medical profession.

'I know it's hard being away', she says, gently, when he hangs up. 'But you'll meet him soon enough.'

When they speak that evening, his father is agitated; he rants about the younger doctors. 'No good, I tell you', he complains. 'One fellow doesn't know what the Jerusalem Syndrome is and another doesn't know the treatment for... for... hyperekplexia. They don't make them like they used to.'

The next day, he recounts the conversation to his sister and they laugh, picturing their father driving the young medics crazy with his quizzing.

The days are fluid, melding into one another like the gooey desserts he's learned to bake.

'Do we need more flour?' she asks while preparing a grocery list for their weekly shopping.

'No, but some sour cream perhaps... and brie', he replies.

When he calls his father that evening, he asks to speak with the nurses too.

He checks if they have enough supplies. If they are taking adequate precautions given his father's advanced age and vulnerability. They assure him that they are, telling him what he wants to hear.

Later, she checks on their house help. Asks for her bank details so she can wire her salary.

'My son knows all that, madam, and he's stuck in our village. I don't know how to operate the ATM', the maid informs her.

'I hope you've stocked up on food, then?' she asks.

'Where, madam. We live from one day to the next.'

'They are distributing food packets. Don't worry', she assures her.

On the pavement outside, a boy drinks water from a large can. The pavement dwellers have spread themselves out, as if claiming ownership of the open road and the sky above. They have befriended a stray dog that sits close to them, wagging its tail.

The scooterists arrive late that day, distracting the crows with the cooked food in their open basket. The birds mill about the basket like vultures; the men flap their arms to shoo them away. The activity draws the attention of the pavement families who begin to sprint towards the men, elbowing each other out of the way like athletes playing foul.

The first to reach emerges victorious, with his meal wrapped in newspaper in one hand and a steaming hot cup of chai (or coffee) in the other. The children dance a little jig of joy. One child sacrifices a few morsels for the dog that bounds up to him, wagging its tail wildly.

A feeling of lethargy sets in.

The first few days had felt like a gift. Like added time that seemed to stretch the year, slow down the earth's rotations and revolution. They had scrambled to make the most of it, cleaning, cooking, sifting through old photos, filing away important papers, and catching up on reading, movies and calls with people they had long lost touch with. Throughout, work had kept them sane, a thread of continuity that seemed to hold together their old way of life with this suspended state of inaction. Now, there is the danger of taking this state of limbo for granted.

The scooterists stop coming with the food packets and the pavement dwellers lie listlessly under their tree, picking at their hair and noses. A man stops by on his evening walk to feed the stray.

No sooner has he laid the meal before the dog than they hurl abuses at him, causing him to quicken his pace. They swoop down and snatch the food—a roti and raw meat—from the confused animal. The dog emits a low growl, then starts barking madly. They throw stones in its direction; it shies and runs off, casting sad backward glances at them. Perhaps its newfound attachment to the pavement dwellers prevents it from showing further aggression.

Then one day, they disappear. It is only when the pavement glistens in the light of the midday sun, freshly hosed down and sanitised, that he notices their absence.

'They must have gone to the migrant camps', she muses. She dials their maid.

'There are no food packets being distributed here, madam', says the maid. 'But I have some biscuits left for the children, and my neighbours are kind.'

His father no longer takes his calls. Any communication between them is strictly through the nurses who are already overburdened with work.

It was his father's wish that they find him a care home, one managed by medical staff, in the environment he was most familiar with. The deterioration had been gradual and the slow progression of Alzheimer's disease had been largely self-diagnosed. He had worked at the hospital for as long as he could until the management decided that it was too risky.

'I know how this progresses', he had told his children. 'It's not pretty.'

He had insisted on a medical environment for reasons of health, he said, but they suspected it was to prolong the association with his profession. Work, for him, had been paramount. It had been the reason for his existence, his raison d'être. Medicine had been his life.

The siblings had looked for appropriate care homes in and around their respective cities. It was an uphill task. They zeroed in on one located on the outskirts of his sister's city and she made sure to visit him every week. He flew down to meet his father whenever he could.

The deterioration had been slow. As a doctor, he was popular with the staff even though he slowed down the nurses and young medics with his constant medical banter and instructions. Prone to bouts of irritability at first, the confusion had set in. And then the delusions.

'Dad thinks he's still a practising doctor, that all the nurses and medics are the staff working for him and the other residents of the home, his patients', his sister had called to tell him.

'What?' he reacted, knowing that the decline had begun.

But they had laughed then, seeing the humour in it together with the sadness.

It was inevitable. Even when forewarned, one is never truly prepared to witness the collapse of a brilliant mind.

His father had taken to giving instructions to all and sundry, diagnosing medical conditions—not always accurate—of fellow residents.

The staff continued to be patient and always accorded him respect by addressing him as 'doctor'.

But now, his sister calls to say that their father no longer recognises her. He does not respond to the names of his wife or parents, all long gone. He no longer responds, she informs her brother, to their own names either.

It is difficult to visit, she says. Both emotionally and practically, given the restrictions.

He had hoped to fly down for his father's birthday but it is impossible now. They must make do with the daily phone calls. Living apart and locked into separate worlds, with memories and without.

She wakes up to him whisking the batter. He adds the egg, butter and sugar, and mixes it all together.

'Mmm. Is that a chocolate cake I smell?' she asks in her morning voice, hugging him from behind.

'The pavement dwellers are back', she observes, as she sips her morning tea by the window.

He wipes his hands on his apron, and joins her by the window to look.

The families are back. The men place fraying straw mats and soiled bed sheets on the pavement. The women rock their babies. A teenager attempts to catch some sleep on a ledge, in the glare of the morning sun. The younger children rub their eyes and snotty noses, and bawl.

His sister calls earlier than usual that day. She is crying.

'Has dad passed away?' he asks, his heart sinking.

'No', she whispers. 'The nurses have baked him a birthday cake.'

That day, it is the head nurse who calls him. His sister has already logged in from her home. The residents of the care home are seated around a table covered with a lace-patterned plastic tablecloth.

He watches as the nurses round up the stragglers; the last of the residents enter the room with measured steps revealing arthritic knees and burdened spines that slow down the pace of the evening.

The nurses wheel in his father. Even at his age, indisposed as he is on his wheelchair, his father has the bearing of his youth. The impassive, creased face belies his confusion upon seeing the crowd. Gnarled fingers grip the handles of the chair. Wispy hair flies with the gust of breeze from a floor fan.

A ward boy enters, smiling broadly. He presents a bouquet of deep red roses to the old man. A nurse brings in the cake, holding it carefully so as not to smudge the icing. *Happy 90th Birthday, Doctor*, says the vanilla-flavoured sugar.

The nurses lead, by clapping and singing enthusiastically. The residents follow suit. *Happy burd-day to you, happy burd-day dear doctor*, they sing off-key, clapping and swaying their heads from side to side.

When his father has cut the cake, aided by a nurse, and the guests given their share of this and other treats, they hang up.

'Look who's on the phone, singing for you!' the nurse had said to his father, adopting the tone of an adult speaking with a child, pointing towards the phone as she spoke.

But he had stared blankly, failing to recognise his children.

They stand by the window observing the pavement dwellers in silence. He stubs his cigarette and returns to the kitchen to check on the cake. Not bad for the first time, he thinks to himself, and looks for a box to place it in.

The pavement dwellers are seated in a circle, huddled together. She cannot tell if they are playing cards or partaking of a meal.

She starts upon spotting him on the road. Cradling a makeshift box crafted from a paper bag, he approaches the street children with the gait of an uncle bringing a treat. They break out of the huddle and descend upon the cake.

He glances up towards the window and waves.

A police jeep drives past on its daily round. *Aat raha*, says the police officer, into the loudspeaker. *Stay indoors.*

The Sweechoos

Gayatri Gill

Ram

'Sweechoos', it's a word you know—legit. Our didi ji made it up. All by herself, too. There's little she manages to do by herself, but inventing words is one of her special gifts, especially when it comes to fabricating endearments that mean little, much like her. Neelam Mehra or didi ji (as she likes to be called by us sweechoos) was unique I'd always thought, but then my opinion, like that of countless others like me, is meaningless, much like the endearments didi ji came up with.

I'd worked at her home for over a decade, doubling up as a cook and driver. The family's regular man Friday. And they treated us well enough by the standards ascribed. Made the kids call us 'bhaaya ji' or 'didi' as the case may be, in return for the salutations we offered them. This sort of strange 'equalised' power play made her feel more connected to her 'sweechoos', the mini army of menial helpers created by Gandhi ji's head to serve her and her ilk.

The word 'bhaaya ji' that the Mehra kids used mustn't be confused with the UP-waala 'bhaiyya'. This was a special sort of 'bhaaya' with an extra 'a' that needed to be rolled around the mouth and dunked in aristocratic saliva before being spit out—oh so gently. It needed its vowels well-oiled like all the fancy cars the Mehras owned. I miss them you know—sort of. After all, they'd been my family away from home for so long, especially didi ji whom I think of very often. Sometimes even with fondness.

With brittle, curling hair that coils like serpents over the odourless flowers of her designer kaftaans, Neelam Mehra is difficult to forget. As is the nasty nasal voice she used to shout out orders to us incessantly, all the bloody time. But it isn't her voice that makes her unforgettable or even her gorgeous skin-deep beauty—what makes her truly unforgettable is the way she smells. The scent of her body doesn't come out of a bottle bought off a shelf. Her smell is unique, and it courses through her blood.

Musky. Powerful. Rich.

The Rich, you see, smell of rich. It's an odour their bodies are born with; even their sweat reeks wealth. Maybe that's why they say that affluence and class run through their bloodlines just as the abject lack of it runs through ours.

I watch the Sea of Humanity that I'm swimming through sighing and shaking as it battles through yet another night of dark despair. The rancid stench of poverty hangs above us all like a giant black cloud swollen with acid rain that's just waiting to burst. Most sweechoos who sleep beside me had come from Tamil Nadu, many months ago. Cheap labour that had come to work at the city's metro construction site much before the lockdown began or anyone knew of a 'corona' other than the one that didi ji and saab drank. But the sweechoos housed in this camp don't all belong to one state. There are people here from Bihar and Odisha, Rajasthan and Bengal. Over 1,500 migrant workers on last count. An inherent swab of our country represented in a hellhole. I'd heard today that at least fifteen of the women here were pregnant. The authorities assured us that they were arranging for special trains to get us home and once again we believed them because isn't that what sweechoos do best? They Listen.

Loud screams suddenly cut through the silence.

There's an explosion of words outside.

Commotion.

Not one person. It's a crowd.

A surging ocean of cries.

Lashing out.

The cops rush out to see what is wrong. They're holding lathis, some of them even have guns. Hey Ram! Don't tell me it's begun. Not here. Not now. We're almost home. A man runs in. He has no face. 'I am Ram', the faceless man says, 'In You am I. We are One. Done with our listening. Now will be their turn. Come on. Wake up!' He urges us in an alarmingly quiet tone and the sleeping colony of despair suddenly begins to stir. Coiling and uncoiling in their sleep like the snakes resting on didi ji's flowery dress. We, the sweechoos.

Now when I look back I realise that perhaps this word does have a hidden meaning after all. I just hadn't thought of it before. Maybe it was born when a good, innocent word 'sweet' (described as 'a small piece of boiled sugar, often sold in a packet' by the Oxford Dictionary) copulated viciously with a particularly unpleasant Hindi expletive (roughly meaning 'vagina'), under a horribly dark starless moon. And of this adulterous union this bastard most horrid was born—the 'sweechoo'. A sweet fool meant to follow orders without question his whole wretched life through. Yes, perhaps didi ji had been right all along. This word does describe us well.

However, it now looked like the sweechoos were finally beginning to rise.

Samara

'Today's Special Lockdown Recipe—the Original Chicken Penang Curry.' 'Yummm', thought Samara, as she peered into her phone, scrolling through Neelam Mehra's Instagram feed. 'How has she managed to get galangal? Certainly not a lockdown essential is it? Spiteful. Shhh. Calm down you!' she whispered to herself as she carefully slipped out of the stiff white cotton sheets that lined her bed, and leisurely pulled on her organic linen dressing gown over her organic block print nightie. There was no need to hurry. No deadlines to meet, just another lazy lockdown morning that stretched languidly into a day filled with endless possibilities. Life sure was good.

'Reshma, mera adrak-haldi chai, please', she murmured into the intercom, 'Thanks, sweechoo', she continued, her morning voice dipped in honey-soaked huskiness. Trademark Samara Malhotra. After all, nothing but perfection worked for her. Wife to one of the top industrialists in the country and a generous philanthropist in her own right, Samara was born with the quintessential diamond encrusted spoon tucked firmly in her mouth. This wasn't her fault, but the weight of this cross, no matter how heavy, was hers alone to bear.

Samara carefully tiptoed past her sleeping husband, the 'Mountain Man', as she had taken to calling him ever since Lockdown 1.0 began. He hadn't stepped down from their third-floor bedroom in three months and, in a way, she didn't blame him. With its unlimited air conditioning, endless supplies of digital entertainment and massive stretches of silence, the 'Adults Only Third-Floor Zone' was highly addictive. The night before had been harsh—he'd hardly slept, binging on *The Handmaid's Tale*; he had wrapped up three seasons of the series in three days flat. Ten and a half hours of content per season spread across three days. About thirty-two hours. Okay, let's round it off to about thirty-six hours in all (for easier calculation). That's one and a half days of being glued to the television screen with no breaks at all. Unreal. Would've been impossible if they had still been living in their 'old' normal, but barring the first few weeks of teething trouble, the Malhotras had adjusted to this 'new' normal quite perfectly. Life truly had moved on and they were all beginning to find beauty in the ordinary.

The kids got ready every morning, wearing their school shirts over their night pyjamas, and with scrubbed faces and well-combed hair, they sat down for their daily classes online. An average of three hours in a virtual classroom coupled with a few home assignments and the permitted two hours of screen time took care of their lockdown days quite well. There were no playgrounds or extracurricular classes taking place outdoors, so most after-school activities had also shifted online. Even the NBA was now doing online basketball coaching. Samara knew this because her son Jehaan had insisted on getting enrolled. He was the school's star basketball player after all, and most of his friends had joined too. Samara, though, had put her foot down. 'Wasteful spending', especially during the lockdown, was a strict no-no.

Times were tough and Ajanta Locks—which had more than 15,000 employees on its payroll—was bracing for the worst. 'Keep the Essentials. Cut the frills', was the Mountain Man's constant refrain since the day Lockdown 1.0 began. She had listened, and they'd let the frills go. All of them. While the permanent office staff had been paid salaries with partial cuts for the first two months, the temps and contractual workers were laid off immediately. There was a lot of anguish but nothing could be done. Locks were out of production; everyone was home protecting whatever they may have otherwise locked in. Ram, her man Friday and cook, had been a victim of the many 'frill' casualties. 'Should've kept him on!' cursed Samara to herself for the thousandth time while sipping her hot haldi chai and scrolling through Neelam Mehra's Insta feed.

Ting!

> New Update: Midnight Munchies
> Fresh mango meringues anyone? A bit untidy but
> who cares! True beauty lies in small imperfections!!
> #mylockdowndiaries

'Balls! The bitch got her Ram to beat the eggs! Imperfect my ass!' thought Samara as she glared at the perfect mango-streaked peaks now being smothered by heart and thumbs up emojis. 'Ohhh!! How I hate her and bloody Insta and everything in between... Okay, caaalm downnn and... breeeath...' she reprimanded herself before silencing her phone and putting it aside. There was a reason that her spirit guru always warned her against getting on social media too early in the day. It always messed up her mind–body balancing chakras and made her feel blue. And if regular days had been bad, COVID had made things even worse. The lockdown showcased talent and everyone was performing. 'Max the day or get the blip out!' became the mantra for survival, and she for one wasn't giving up!

'A good comeback. That's all I need. Eject negativity. Exhaaale... Oooh! The blue birds are chirping, aren't they? Looks like gorgeous summer is truly here.'

Ram

The heat—ruthless, unforgiving, relentless, stretching endlessly before us. Above and below, it explodes like mini volcanos of helplessness, erupting no matter which way we go. We'd started our trudge home more than seven weeks ago. Walked about a hundred kilometres before the accident on KMP Highway halted us in our tracks. Five sweechoos had been mowed down and eight injured by a truck, some fifteen kilometres away from where we were. One of the dead had been just a year old. That's the first time we were stopped and told that getting anywhere by foot was life threatening. The authorities had detained us in a makeshift camp on the road for a good ten days before we managed to get permission to move again.

I'd called didi ji that day even before I dialled my wife, but she told me quite curtly that I couldn't come back. 'Gone too far now, Ram', she'd said. And the authorities couldn't let us go either because we still had miles to go before we reached our villages. Catch-22. Like that cheesy advertisement for Amul chocolate I'd heard a long time ago. 'Too old for tricycles, too young to be a pilot.' 'But I think you're just right for Amul chocolate', crooned the beautiful girl in the ad. Neerja, that had been her name. She's the one who was martyred saving some kids from hijackers on a plane a few years after she did that ad. I know because I watched a movie about her in a multiplex with recliners (first day first show). Five hundred rupees for a single ticket is what it cost me but that was an occasional luxury I allowed myself back when I had a job. Hey Ram! What I wouldn't do, to get a piece of that chocolate right now!

When I look back now, I'm not sure what drove me to it. Maybe it was that same Amul ad playing on someone's phone during a rerun of the old *Mahabharat* while we waited for the authorities to decide what they would do with us. Or perhaps it was the small chocolate poking out of the cop's square pocket, right under his name badge. Or maybe I was just sick to the belly and couldn't bear this uncertainty anymore.

I'd been shunted out of two camps already, with their unlimited supply of sick-looking green water and one-meal-a-day food plan. I was done with it. We all were, I guess. 'Either they let us get to our homes or we get into theirs. Simple.' That's what I told the people at my camp and they listened. Even harder than I'd believed. Their anger ran deep, as did mine. How could it be otherwise? Some of them had been on the road for more than three months! Since the day a train meant to get them home had ghosted them in Mumbai, a city they had once called their home. I watched quietly as their grief melted deftly into a burning rage against a system that never seemed to work. Against the people who forever told them what was wrong. Their rage grew before me and fathered its own form. It had birthed from a mere flicker, but now it roared with hunger. It would stop only when its belly was full. When it had had its due.

I lit that flame when I snatched the lathi from the cop trying to herd us into yet another camp. This one complimenting itself on having once been a sprawling racecourse where well-bred horses had run. The cop had tried to argue with me, said our home states had given them new diktats. Apparently now the healthy didn't want us back. We were to be kept out of city limits. He didn't realise how fast the desperation in our eyes could transform into shock and fear as I smashed the lathi on his head with all my might. Hard.

A squiggly stream of blood flowed down from his cracked skull. It smelt poor, much like mine.

I read the name on his badge. He had been a Ram too.

Maybe I should call her again, my didi ji before the Rams begin to run loose.

Samara

#KarishmaKhannaCovidCupboard
#LockdownInnovativeInventions
#GlamOnMagazine2020
#GoodIdeasAtHome #StaySafeStayHome

Karishma Khanna was one of Samara's favourite social influencers and her 'Lockdown Ideas for Everything' hacks were legendary. Her previous post, 'The COVID Cupboard', had just featured fourth in the 'Lockdown Innovative Inventions Top 20' list of *GlamOn* magazine, and Samara never missed any of her posts.

Today's is about using night cream in the day to boost skin rejuvenation. Apparently, night cream is much more powerful than its day counterpart and using it both day and night is now the worst kept lockdown secret! 'This woman is sooo lit!' Samara smiles to herself, sending many hearts and flames flying straight to Karishma's timeline while reposting it on her page. 'This is inspirational stuff, the kind that doesn't try showing anyone up. Just the type of comeback I should think up… hmmm…'

And just as she begins framing her response, typing each word with utmost care, her phone starts to ring. Exasperated, she sees that it is Ram calling again, one of the Rams she had let go just when the lockdown began. She cuts the call. Can't talk worker woes early morning, she thinks, I'll call him later in the day, first thing. And then, with a contented sigh, she settles in to gather her thoughts while watching the blue birds in the verandah sing.

The bullet whizzes in right then. Samara falls to the floor. Red is the colour of the hot blood gushing out of the world's most perfect circular hole. The neatest fountain of blood she creates, and it smells of the rich.

Neelam Mehra, Karishma Khanna and Samara Malhotra's kin all over the country watch in horror as their whole world begins to cave in.

The COVID Cupboard

Karishma Khanna's 'COVID cupboard' idea is simple but packs a punch. Rather than operating from her full-scale walk-in wardrobe, Karishma used her mind and downgraded to one small special cupboard in the first week of the lockdown itself. 'The COVID cupboard', as she calls it, 'is filled with clothes I've never worn, but have always wanted to. Comfortable, loose, cool day clothes and a bunch of sexy nightwear.'

Advantages?
No wasting time browsing through your entire collection before deciding what you want to wear to stay home. Plus, once the lockdown ends you can pack away your special COVID collection and donate it to the needy.

'Aam ke aam guthliyon ke daam', she chuckles.

Challenges?
'So, I had initially planned on giving my COVID clothes to the squatters down the street, but some "friends" told me they've gone. The roads are bereft of the homeless

and the poor; I mean there aren't even any beggars left. All had been packed into trains and sent home, or put away in some state-run camps outside city borders. Essential, I guess, in these times, to keep the city folk safe. I was disappointed, but didn't let the detractors get the better of me.

'Figured if the squatters and beggars (bless their souls) never returned, I'd just make dust cloths of my COVID clothes. Or, maybe, send them off to orphanages. There will always be orphans in the world, won't there?' she beams.

The eternal optimist in Karishma believes she will cross that bridge when she comes to it. After all, no good deed ever goes unpunished. Someone, somewhere is waiting to receive from her. Of that she is sure.

And so are we.

For now, Karishma has let go of all her Rams and is using this time to detox and explore parts of herself she'd never known existed. Dancing, playing the piano, baking, and painting the most complex designs on ceramics. 'Maybe one of these will fuel a future business idea, who knows? For the brave new world of tomorrow holds in its womb a limitless puddle of opportunities. And I for one am just getting started', signs off the vivacious mother of a naughty one-year old.

Congratulations again, Karishma Khanna on being featured in the 'Lockdown Innovative Inventions Top 20' list. *GlamOn* magazine and its partner groups are proud to be associated with you.

We're watching you girl!

More power to staying happy, staying in.

#StayHome #StaySafe
#NoPlaceBetterThanHome

Updated June 2021

Karishma was right about her COVID collection. Her COVID clothes did get used.

Designer body bags were made of them.

We at *GlamOn* salute every life lost in the 2020 pandemic riots.

#StayHome #StaySafe

Today is Tomorrow

Julia Prendergast

I love running but I'm sick of running. Between the meetings and to break the work, I run. I could stop doing it, only I'm desperate for the after-feeling, like the old world is still possible. The feeling is full and then empty, like things I don't want to draw attention to, here. Am I running to or from? Suddenly running feels empty. Full-empty. What does that even mean? The world is losing meaning.

In the first weeks of isolation, I looked forward to the meetings. Now I hate them. I love-hate them, like running. In the virtual gatherings I see me as others see me, literally not figuratively. I see my (not virtual) background—the dressing table with the long mirror. In the mirror I see my bed. I see the bed in real time if I look forward, beyond my screen, and I see it in the mirror background, behind me. It looks like a scene I'm trying to write, a temporally shifty scene that's not working yet. It's a side effect of the virus. Dissolving time. Future past. Or, past future. Is there a difference?

It's night-time. The energy picks up as the daylight fades. People emerge from their rooms as if something is going to happen, but it's only dinner and that was hours ago, now. I answer a few more emails, messages from across the seas where it's still yesterday. I'm taken with the idea of talking to yesterday, in real time. I should go to sleep except I'm not tired—I'm not even slightly sleepy. I should have run twice today. I should have gone harder, faster, to and away from.

I stare at the laptop screen. In my background two lamps flank the dressing table, one stained-glass, the other hand-painted pottery with a textured lampshade, like shifting tidemarks on the sand. I long for the sea, but so what? People are dying. The base of the lamp has swirl markings in green and clay-yellow, painted swirls, and etchings in the swirls, like teeth marks. The teeth marks belong to another story, but the loss of meaning and the emptying of time blends stories. The lamp with the swirl markings looks like ancient Greek pottery, like wind and teeth in paint and clay, like the Trojan women, wailing. When she gave it to me, she said: 'If I'd known it was a lamp, rather than a vase, I mightn't have given it to you so readily… See the hole', she adds, 'for the cord?' There is an old perfume bottle, too, on the dressing table, also hers. The glass is textured, refracting lamplight, pinging amber.

At night-time, if I stare at the screen, it's like I'm in a meeting. I can see my background in the screen's reflection, just like my framed face, at the meetings. I join a meeting from the future to see if I'm right, to check if it really does look the same.

The host says: 'You're the only one in the meeting.'

'I know', I say. 'I know.' I laugh but it's not really that funny.

Is the platform the host? I think so. I decide the platform is the host and I am the organiser. I wish the host would bring me another glass of champagne. I don't like the hallway at night.

I read my stories aloud, in this room, and now I'm talking to the host, who is a platform. If my children are awake, beyond the door, they will think I am the madwoman in the attic.

In the daytime, I like the hallway. It's cluttered with things people have shifted out of their bedrooms. A small bin, painted wire—a large cushion with a frayed edge, split, duck down scattered like the soft feathers of dead ducks. I think the feathers should stay there until we have a vaccine—I spill a few more out. 'Why are you doing that?' he asks.

Each day there are new things in the hallway—a school bag, defunct (I take it as a statement against home-schooling). I refrain from comment because I don't care and I don't want to discuss the pile—it's like a social experiment except the pandemic is real and it brings stuff out of people's bedrooms and into the hallway. He adds a kettle to the pile (it's a perfectly good kettle—he bought a new one and he is very pleased about it—he is not a buyer of unnecessary things). I think about it while the kettle boils. I wonder what it means, precisely.

Who is to say what is useful now and what's not? Or, what means something? Or whether meaning is altogether necessary? I'm interested in the things in the hallway as individual objects, but more so collectively. I want to add a curveball, something useful and meaning-heavy, but I'm too interested in observing. I don't want to interfere with what's happening in the hallway.

In effect I started it. I put two long, timber sitting benches there, from under my bed. I cleaned the wooden floorboards by hand with fig-scented spray. I needed my workspace to smell nice. I didn't bring the benches back because people started adding on, as if this were a thing, like a garage sale in our hallway.

Sometimes, at night, I walk from room to room and listen to their breathing. With some of them, I can get really close without invading their dreams, so close I can feel the vibrations of their breath, like when they were babies. I walk from room to room, collecting their breathing. I know how lucky I am to have breathing people in my house, a whole collection of breathing people, only at night-time their breathing seems louder than it really is. It's like I can hear it when I'm not close enough to hear it. It bothers me and so I get up close to their breathing to remind myself it's real. Later, I stand in the hallway of unused things and I put their breathing together in my mind.

I go back to my desk because words make things meaningful—words collect objects as a composite picture that makes some kind of sense; even refracted sense is okay because of the work of association. Only today I can't make the words breathe and I feel that the hallway is without associations and, at the same time, over-laden. It's too much. I go back to the hallway and listen for things I shouldn't be able to hear. I wish I was a horse so I could stand here all night. I could sleep (not-sleep), standing in medias res, among the things we're letting go of.

I should go to bed; it's late enough, after midnight. I open my calendar to check tomorrow for front-facing meetings. Twelve-thirty and four o'clock. 'Go to sleep you idiot', I say, holding my arms, firmly and kindly, as if I'm someone else, which, to be fair, I kind-of am.

In the beginning, I made my bed for the meetings. Feigning order. I'm not a bed-maker. I've never really seen the point. Now, I make the bed only sometimes. To some extent, it depends on who's in the meeting. I'm not in the mood for meetings anymore. Things have shifted. Meetings are so yesterday. I'll perk up tomorrow, no worries. I'll run first thing, wash my hair, put a fresh bra on—not this sweaty sports bra. I take a black lacy one, hang it over my chair, in readiness. It will make me feel better, I think. It's a champagne thought, black lace ridiculousness. In the night-time light, with the lamps and the candle, it's like I'm inside a kaleidoscope, colours pinging, hurtling towards me from multiple directions. I'm not seeing them so much as feeling them. It's true. I'm not making this up. It's not the champagne.

I respond to my friend from across the seas. 'I'll sort that out tomorrow', I say. 'It's 2 AM', I add. 'Today is tomorrow. It's a good title for a short story…' I've barely pushed send and he comes back: 'OK. I love that title—who's gonna use it first?'

'We both are', I say. 'Seriously. I'm going to have a crack at it tomorrow.' As I lay my head on the pillow, I remember today is tomorrow and that means I should have a crack at it now but, finally, I'm tired.

Today is tomorrow and I'm in a meeting. It's so annoying—being in meetings with yourself. In the dressing table mirror I can see my bed, because looking forward is looking back, now… I rarely make the bed now because time is for other things and it's night-time somewhere. If perchance I am one of those who will die, sooner rather than later, I want to spend my time doing things that feel like they have a point. Not bed-making. I don't want to see myself, anymore, in this stupid fucking meeting. I reach for the mouse, blank my image. I subscribe to the chat on the side, a conversation in writing. 'Connectivity issues', I type. I think it's, perhaps, the truest thing I've written across this empty-full time, where today is tomorrow, a forwards-backwards yesterday, but for words.

About the Authors

Editors

Meenakshi Bharat is a writer, translator, reviewer and cultural theorist who teaches at the University of Delhi. Her writing, both creative and critical, has been spurred by contemporary concerns. This includes numerous books, articles, and short stories, both for children and adults. Her love of the short story form has taken her to co-editing four successful Indo-Australian short fiction anthologies, including the latest *Glass Walls: Stories of Tolerance and Intolerance.*

Sharon Rundle is a member of the Institute of Professional Editors, and Chair of the UTS Writers' Alumni. She has co-edited four anthologies of short fiction from Australia and South Asia. Her stories, essays and articles have appeared in books, anthologies, journals and magazines including: *Claiming Space: Australian Women Writers*; *Transnational Literature*; *Southerly*; *Indo-Australian Relations: Retrospective and Prospective*; and *Encounters: Modern Australian Short Stories.*

Contributing authors

Alex Cothren's writing has been published or is forthcoming in *Meanjin, Island, Overland Online, The Conversation* and *Australian Book Review*. He won the 2013 Carmel Bird Award and the 2021 William Van Dyke Short Story Prize. 'Let's Talk Trojan Bee' was the winner of the 2019 Peter Carey Short Story Award.

Andrew Kwong won the 2021 Michael Crouch Award for a Debut Work for *One Bright Moon*, a memoir about his life in China as a young child during the Great Chinese Famine of the late 1950s and early 60s and the Great Leap Forward, and his move to Australia. He works as a family physician in New South Wales, Australia.

Anne Benjamin is an Australian writer with strong links to India. Her memoir, *Saffron and Silk*, recalls her years in Chennai and explores themes such as intercultural marriage, motherhood, poverty, religion, society and development. Her books include *Gemstones* (an anthology of collaborative tanka poetry) and *Not Forgotten: Australian Catholic Educators 1820–2020* (co-edited with Seamus O'Grady).

Bashabi Fraser CBE is a poet, writer, translator, and the Chief Editor of the international e-journal *Gitanjali and Beyond*. She is Professor Emerita of English and Creative Writing, and Director, Scottish Centre of Tagore Studies, at Edinburgh Napier University. Her many awards include the Outstanding Woman of Scotland (2015) and the AIO Prize for Literary Services in Scotland (2009).

Cate Kennedy's novel *The World Beneath* won the People's Choice Award in the 2010 NSW Premier's Literary Awards. She has published collections of short fiction (*Dark Roots* and *Like a House on Fire*) and poetry (*Signs of Other Fires*, *Joyflight*, and *The Taste of River Water*). Her work has won the Steele Rudd Award, the Age Short Story Award, and the Vincent Buckley Poetry Prize.

Devika Brendon, educator, reviewer, journalist and writer, has served as Consultant Editor of *FemAsia* magazine, and is a member of the editorial board of *New Ceylon Writing*, a literary journal. Her poetry and short stories have been published in journals and anthologies in India, Sri Lanka, Australia, Italy and Africa.

Eugen Bacon's speculative fiction, poetry and nonfiction has won or been nominated for several awards, including the British Science Fiction Association Award, the Bridport Prize, the Copyright Agency Prize, the Australian Shadows Award, the Ditmar Award, and the Nommo Award for Speculative Fiction by Africans. Bacon's creative work has appeared in literary and speculative fiction publications worldwide.

Gayatri Gill is a producer, scriptwriter, story editor and co-founder of Swastik Productions, Mumbai, with over fifteen years of writing and production experience across television, digital, animation and documentary formats. *The Day Before Today: Lockdown Stories* is her debut collection of short fiction.

Gulzar, lyricist, poet, author, screenwriter and film director, was awarded the Padma Bhushan in 2004, the third-highest civilian award in India. He has won the Sahitya Akademi Award, the Dadasaheb Phalke Award (the highest award in Indian cinema), several National Film Awards (India), an Academy Award, and a Grammy Award. Gulzar directed the films *Aandhi* and *Mausam*, and the television series *Mirza Ghalib* and *Kirdaar*.

Janhavi Acharekar has authored a novel, *Wanderers, All*; a collection of short stories, *Window Seat: Rush-hour Stories from the City*; and a travel guide, *Moon Mumbai & Goa*. She is a contributing editor at *Conde Nast Traveller India*. A 2009 Charles Wallace Fellow, her features on travel, books and the arts have appeared in leading publications in India, the UK and Canada.

Julia Prendergast is a Senior Lecturer (Writing and Literature), and Academic Director, Pathways and Partnerships, at Swinburne University, Melbourne. She is the author of the novel *The Earth Does Not Get Fat*, and her short stories feature in many anthologies and journals. She is Chair of the Australasian Association of Writing Programs, and a supporter of transdisciplinary, open and collaborative research practices.

Kate Grenville AO has published many novels including *Lilian's Story*, *The Secret River*, *The Lieutenant*, and *A Room Made of Leaves*, some of which have been adapted for the screen and stage. She has won several awards, such as the Vogel Literary Award, the Orange Prize for Fiction, and the Commonwealth Writers' Prize. She received a Lifetime Achievement in Literature award from the Australia Council.

Matthew Lupton is a songwriter, musician, and a vinyl record collector. He handles customer experience and webmaster duties at his family's auto business.

Mitra Phukan is an Assamese writer, translator and columnist. She is the author of the novels *The Collector's Wife* and *A Monsoon of Music*; a volume of short stories, *A Full Night's Thievery*; and four children's books, among other works. She has also translated several important works of Assamese authors. Her own works have been translated into several languages.

Niharika Chibber Joe is a prize-winning poet and a short story writer. She writes in English, and occasionally in Japanese and Hindi. Born and raised in India, she now lives in the United States where she works in public diplomacy for the US government.

Priya Sarukkai Chabria is an award-winning poet, translator and writer whose books include *Andal: The Autobiography of a Goddess* (translation), *Sing of Life: Revisioning Tagore's Gitanjali* (poetry), *Clone* (speculative fiction), and *Bombay/Mumbai: Immersions* (nonfiction). She is the founding editor of *Poetry at Sangam*, and has collaborated with photographers, filmmakers and dancers.

Rashida Murphy is the author of the novel *The Historian's Daughter*, and the short story collection *The Bonesetter's Fee and Other Stories*. Her stories, essays and poetry have been published in many anthologies and international literary journals. She works as a mentor to emerging writers of colour, runs workshops on anti-colonial writing, and has served as a judge for literary competitions and awards.

Shirley Hazzard worked for the United Nations throughout much of the 1950s. She wrote award-winning novels and nonfiction books, including a memoir of her friendship with Graham Greene. Her novel *The Great Fire* won the 2003 US National Book Award for Fiction, the Miles Franklin Award, the William Dean Howells Medal, and was named a Book of the Year by *The Economist*.

Sujata Sankranti taught at the University of Delhi where she retired as Associate Professor. She has published a volume of short stories and a novel, *In the Shadow of Legends*. Many of her short stories have appeared in journals and anthologies in India and abroad, and she was the global Commonwealth Short Story Prize winner for the year 1998.

Sunil Badami has been published in every major media outlet in Australia, including *The Sydney Morning Herald*, *The Australian*, *The Guardian*, *The Monthly*, *The Drum Online*, *Art + Australia*, *Australian Gourmet Traveller* and more, including the prestigious literary journals *Southerly*, *Island*, *Meanjin* and *Westerly*. His work has been anthologised in Australia and overseas.

Susanne Gervay OAM is recognised for her writings on social justice and for her acclaimed short stories. Her literature for children and young adults seeks to empower youth and to oppose the spread of bigotry, and is endorsed by many organisations. She was awarded the Order of Australia for her contribution to children's literature, and the International Literacy Association's Lifetime Literature Award.

Tony Birch is the author of *Ghost River* (winner of the Victorian Premier's Prize for Indigenous Writing), *The White Girl* (winner of the NSW Premier's Award for Indigenous Writing), and short story collections such as *Father's Day*, *The Promise* and *Common People*. He was awarded the 2017 Patrick White Award, and is a frequent contributor to ABC local radio and Radio National shows.

Yasmine Gooneratne AO has received Sri Lanka's Sahithya Rathna lifetime achievement award and the Order of Australia for her contributions to literature and education. A novelist, poet, and teacher of English literature, she is the Patron of the Jane Austen Society of Australia. *A Change of Skies*, her first novel, won the 1991 Marjorie Barnard Literature Award for Fiction.

Acknowledgements

Shirley Hazzard, 'The Flowers of Sorrow', from *Collected Stories*, by Shirley Hazzard, edited by Brigitta Olubas, with a Foreword by Zoë Heller. Copyright © 2020 by the Estate of Shirley Hazzard Steegmuller. Reprinted by permission of Farrar, Straus and Giroux and the Little, Brown Book Group Ltd, UK. All rights reserved.

Eugen Bacon, 'Unlimited Data', in *Cyberfunk! Anthology,* edited by Milton J Davis, pp 42–46, Georgia: MVMedia LLC, 2021. Reproduced with permission of publishers and the author.

Gulzar, 'Najoom', translated into English by Masooma Ali in *Raavi Paar and Other Stories*, pp 48–53, New Delhi: Rupa Publications, 2010. Reproduced with permission of Gulzar, Adil Ali and the publishers.

Alex Cothren, 'Let's Talk Trojan Bee', *Meanjin,* Spring 2019, Melbourne University Publishing. Reproduced with permission of the author.

Tony Birch, 'Party Lights', in *Common People,* Queensland: University of Queensland Press, 2017. Reproduced with permission of publishers and the author.

Sharon Rundle, 'Kiewa Creek Diary', in *Seeds and Skeletons: The 30th UTS Writers' Anthology*. New South Wales: Brio Books, 2016. Reproduced with permission of publishers and the author.

Cate Kennedy, 'Direct Action', in *Dark Roots,* Copyright © 2006 by Cate Kennedy. Reproduced with permission of Scribe Publications, Grove Atlantic Inc and the author.

Kate Grenville, 'A Room Made of Leaves', in *A Room Made of Leaves,* pp 306–317, Copyright © Kate Grenville, 2020. Reproduced with permission of Canongate Books, Text Publishing and the author.

Yasmine Gooneratne, 'A Little Light Reading', adapted from *A Change of Skies*, Sydney, Pan Macmillan Publishers, 1991. Reproduced with permission of the author.

Rashida Murphy, 'Talking Beasts', in *The Bonesetter's Fee and Other Stories*, Sydney: Spineless Wonders, 2021. Reproduced with permission of publishers and the author.

Sunil Badami, 'Something's Gotta Give', *Meanjin*, Autumn, Vol 68, No 1, pp 161–168, Melbourne: Melbourne University Press, 2009. Reproduced with permission of the author.

Janhavi Acharekar, 'Learning to Bake', *Transnational Literature*, Vol 13, October. Bath Spa University, UK. 2021. Reproduced with permission of the author.

Julia Prendergast, 'Today is Tomorrow', *TEXT*, Vol 24, No 1, April 2020. Australasian Association of Writing Programs. Reproduced with permission of the author.

The Editors would like to thank Roanna Gonsalves for providing an overview of *Relatively True*, the stories, and even the wider context of their series of anthologies of stories from the Indian subcontinent and Australia.